Grief
and
Sexuality

Grief
and
Sexuality

Life After Losing a Spouse

Rachel Nafziger Hartzler

Herald Press
Scottdale, Pennsylvania
Waterloo, Ontario

Library of Congress Cataloging-in-Publication Data
Hartzler, Rachel Nafziger, 1948-
Grief and sexuality : life after losing a spouse / Rachel Nafziger
Hartzler.
    p. cm.
Includes bibliographical references.
ISBN 0-8361-9340-7 (pbk. : alk. paper)
    1. Grief—Religious aspects—Christianity. 2. Spouses—Death—
Religious aspects—Christianity. 3. Dating (Social customs)—Religious
aspects—Christianity. 4. Hartzler, Rachel Nafziger, 1948- I. Title.
    BV4908.H35 2006
    155.9'3708654—dc22   2006015775

Unless otherwise noted, Scripture is from the *New Revised Standard Version Bible*, copyright © 1989 by the Division of Christian Education of the National Council of the Churches of Christ in the USA, and is used by permission, with all rights reserved.

To those from whom I have learned,
whose stories informed, inspired, and encouraged me.

In memory of loved ones whose deaths
precipitated grief journeys,
especially Harold.

Contents

Foreword, by Otto Klassen 9
Preface 11

Part 1: Grief
  1. Loss and Suffering 21
  2. Lament: Responding to Loss and Suffering 51
  3. Learning and Transformation 77

Part 2: Sexuality
  4. Living Well Beyond the Crisis 105
     Relationships Old and New 106
     Attitudes Regarding Sexuality 122
     Celibacy 130

Part 3: Looking Forward
  5. Implications for Pastoral Care 155
     Considerations for Pastoral Care
       of Bereaved People 156
     Ongoing Agenda for Pastoral Caregivers 163
     Learn From Bereaved People 178
     A Plan for Pastoral Care for Bereaved
       Widowed People 187

Conclusion 193

Appendix 197
Annotated Bibliography and Additional Resources . . . 209
Notes 217
The Author 237

Foreword

On Palm Sunday, April 11, 1965, a huge tornado ripped away our house as my wife and I tried to hold down a human pyramid, our four daughters and a neighbor girl. Four years later, the house had been rebuilt when an intruder entered it and murdered my wife, the mother of the four girls.

While the experience of the tornado was at the time dramatic, it left almost no scars at all. But the loss of a spouse by death, the experts tell us repeatedly, is a hurt that can hardly be equaled. Even when we know that the blow is coming, experts also affirm, we cannot prepare for it. It is life changing.

Grieving a loss of a spouse is one of life's most shattering wounds. But why? Half of all of us will experience this trauma, and we know it. The knowledge that we are all going to die is one of the most certain things that binds us together. Why then have we failed to develop better ways to cope with grief, or at least better armor to protect against the hurt?

The sudden and unexpected death of her husband when she was fifty-one not only plunged Rachel Nafziger Hartzler into grievous mourning, it also caused her to change professions. The former obstetrical nurse quit her job, enrolled in seminary and became a pastor.

In *Grief and Sexuality*, her first book, Rachel brings insights from religion and theology to the clinician's eye by generously wrapping the account of her own struggles with spousal grief through a review of a broad range of thinkers about grief, mourning, and mystery.

The reader is the beneficiary. In her discussions about lament she taps the ancient wisdom of the Psalms. She sees in ritual not only the expression of accumulated cultural knowledge, but also the "language of the soul."

Rachel's account opens the possibility of redeeming the intense suffering so typical of spousal grief by looking honestly at grief and finding joy there also. Pain speaks also of spiritual sensitivity, and brings the possibilities of transformation.

Again the material comes to life by being wrapped in the shared account of her grief. Again the reader is the beneficiary.

Admittedly some of her material grew out of scholastic requirements. A questionnaire, which she called the Living Well questionnaire, was sent to 220 widowed people and the results compiled. Hartzler, to the reader's benefit, draws no unwarranted statistical conclusions from this material but finds useful remarks shared by the respondents. In her discussion of the possibility of personal transformation she hints at learning from the unborn fetus.

This reader is reminded of a line from Emily Dickinson: *Parting is all we know of heaven / and all we need of hell.* Perhaps our grief should remind us that when we approach death, like the unborn fetus, we are on the near side of a transformation that is still shrouded in mystery.

> *Otto D. Klassen*
> *Cofounder*
> *Oaklawn Mental Health Center*
> *Goshen, Indiana*

Preface

Unless a grain of wheat falls into the earth and dies,
it remains just a single grain;
but if it dies,
it bears much fruit.
—John 12:24

Love gives life meaning
and life gives us one chance
to learn the meaning of love.
—Richard Rohr[1]

Life is an opportunity for perpetual transformation. We are given life, but we all experience loss from the time we are born. When a baby emerges from a mother's body and the umbilical cord is cut, separation from the mother begins. We experience additional loss with each stage of growth and development, for we cannot enter a new stage of life without leaving something behind. It's not a question of whether a person will experience loss, or even if the losses will be pleasant or unpleasant. Both pleasure and pain are in store for everyone. Perhaps the only significant question is how we will respond.

Nearly everyone will suffer the potentially devastating loss of loved ones in death. Exceptions are perhaps those who die young and those who never love. The good news is that with every loss there is something to be gained. Stories in this book illustrate how, even though the journey may be long and difficult and even though most people never "get over" their great losses, living with loss can lead to something new. Loss creates an opportunity for metamorphosis. It is an invitation to transformation. Even after a grief-laden, life-altering, identity-questioning experience of losing a spouse, one can eventually get to a place of living well again.

My own experiences of loss have been quite ordinary. My father was killed in a truck accident the day before I turned twenty-one. I had a special relationship with him, and his death was a deeply saddening experience. An "invitation" that came to me with my father's death was to become an adult, to become independent—from my father because he had died and from my mother because she was now a widow with four children younger than I. The time was right to become an adult, so although the loss was a life-changing event, it did not devastate me.

Thirty years later, at age fifty-one, I experienced a loss that happens to nearly half of all married people.[2] My spouse died. For a spouse to die is obviously not unusual.[3] My mother had been a widow for thirty years. Like many people I know, she seemed to make adjustments and live well after being widowed. So I had no idea of the horror that accompanies spousal death. I was startled by the depth of pain, the intense upheaval of my identity, and the tremendous adjustments in living that were triggered by the death of my husband, Harold E. Hartzler, on October 6, 1999. I was jolted into the realization that if this was an "ordinary" loss, then ordinary losses are much worse than I ever imagined. I found grief to be a profoundly powerful and provocative confrontational emotion that rudely awakened and catapulted me into a new undesired space.

I felt God's presence with me in my crisis, yet there was a barrier in my communication with God. I had difficulty praying, so others prayed on my behalf. Through their prayers, words, and actions, my caring community extended God's grace to me. My community expanded beyond my family, close friends, and church family to include others who had been widowed or suffered profound loss. I found great support for asking questions and making adjustments. In addition to the support of people, I discovered books and articles that were wonderful sources of information and encouragement. As I talked, listened, and read, I discovered that I was normal.

To work at emerging questions about life and death, to focus on new areas of growth, and to prepare for my then very uncertain future, I began taking classes at Associated Mennonite Biblical Seminary (AMBS).[4] I studied and learned about suffering, spiritual growth, and transformation, and my life took on new and rich meaning.

As time passed, some questions were answered while others were not. New questions emerged about how to live well with the empty spaces in my life and the scars that remained, even as I slowly experienced some healing. In the first years of my seminary work I wrote numerous papers about loss and grief, mourning and healing. I found helpful resources for many of my questions, including conversations with other bereaved people. I became acquainted with many widowed people in seminars and workshops related to loss—first as a participant and then as a leader. As I learned from people who had "been there," I became aware of a vast source of wisdom that had not been well tapped. The idea of making a study of widowhood as part of my thesis project began to emerge.

I compiled a list of 220 people, mostly friends and acquaintances, who are or at one time were widowed, and I designed a questionnaire, which I sent to them. The response was phenomenal! Almost 70 percent—152 people—responded. I was deeply moved and nearly overwhelmed with gratitude for the stories, some extremely personal, that people offered me. I also was honored and humbled by the responses. Reading and assimilating them became holy work for me.

I am truly indebted to all who shared with me in conversation, tears, and laughter, and who responded to the questionnaire. I have attempted to hold the information reverently; I hope and pray that I have lived up to my commitment to use these stories respectfully, carefully, and confidentially.[5]

This study became an opportunity to integrate my studies at AMBS, where I earned a master of arts in Christian formation in 2004. In my research I found materials that address the deep spiritual, theological, and psychological aspects of change that occur within a person who is adjusting to life after the death of a spouse. My studies in Christian formation, pastoral care, biblical theology, human psychological development, and spiritual growth have all included insights that offer some understanding of the tremendous upheaval people encounter in loss and grief. I offer ideas that I hope will be useful for people navigating along a grief journey as well as for those who care for grieving people.

Detailed lists of responses and many actual quotes from the returned questionnaires are presented in my thesis essay, available in the AMBS library under the title *Loss as an Invitation to Transformation: Living Well Following the Death of a Spouse.*

I reviewed a few other empirical studies of bereavement and noted findings consistent with my data. However, the focus of my study seems to be unique. Few studies of widowed people focus on the years beyond the initial grief period.

This book traces issues faced by people following spousal death. I have integrated theoretical understandings, analysis of data from the returned questionnaires along with other observations, personal experience, and introspection.

Chapter 1 begins with a general look at loss as part of the human experience and then focuses specifically on unique issues that confront people after the death of a spouse. Here I summarize demographic data from the empirical study and examine suffering and the question of theodicy—the question of how evil can exist in the world if God is all-powerful and all-loving.

Chapter 2 focuses on lament, a response to loss and suffering. The pattern of biblical laments is articulated and tasks of grief as described by various practitioners are considered.

Chapter 3 explores ways to integrate loss and suffering into life. Included are stories about how people have incorporated loss into their lives, have recognized psychological and spiritual growth, and have even found gifts growing out of grief.

Chapter 4 looks beyond the crisis of loss to the time when a sense of wellness begins to evolve and life's journey continues in new ways. Because little has been written about the *ongoing* agenda of widowed people, I have given extra attention to the topics of this chapter. A big question for many widowed people is how to deal with their sexuality while celibate, how to reconcile intimacy needs with the realities of being single. This is addressed in some detail, including the description of models for celibate sexuality. I consider the apex of this book to come in the section of this chapter entitled "Integration of Sexuality, Heart, Head, and Spirituality." Here I propose a prototype for living well as a single, sexual, and celibate person.

The final chapter offers suggestions for pastoral care and friendship of bereaved people. This chapter is forward-looking, showing how to put into practice what can be learned from the literature and from people who have "been there." I explore models for offering pastoral care, such as the notion of being a "wounded healer" and a "caregiving sage."

An underlying theme of this book is the concept of life as a journey. The focus is on how to live well in spite of the challenges, difficulties, and crises along the way and how to grow through unpleasant, undesirable life experiences. I hope and pray that this study will make a contribution to understandings of personal transformation, which is of key interest to the Christian ministry to which I am committed.

It would be impossible to name all the people who helped make this book possible. Categories of people are my extended family, my wide circle of friends, and members of my congregation who walked with me and prayed with me, who listened to me and shared their stories, and who gave me hope, encouragement, and presence during the stages of my grief journey. At my request, a group of widows encircled me soon after Harold's death and others joined the circle in the years that followed. They include Joy Kauffman King, Elizabeth Gingerich, Ruth Ann Miller Brunk, Elaine Unzicker, Bonnie Blough, Belle Duerkson, Sara VonGunten, and Gale Livengood.

As mentioned above, the 152 people who responded to my questionnaire helped guide my writing in particular ways that give authenticity to this book. Since they responded anonymously, these people can't be named, but you know who you are and I appreciate more than I can say what you have given me.

Special thanks to the dear friends who graciously read my manuscript in various stages and provided valuable feedback: Carole Boshart, Christine Guth, Myra Oswald, J. Lorne Peachey, John D. Rempel, Janet Smucker, Kathleen Stiffney, Everett Thomas, Sara Wengerd, and Janette Yoder. Otto Klassen has honored me by writing the foreword to this book. He is a man with great wisdom, a compassionate heart, and a gentle spirit, and is highly esteemed throughout Elkhart County, Indiana, and beyond as a psychiatrist with the utmost integrity and outstanding clinical and leadership skills.

I am extremely thankful for AMBS faculty, staff, and classmates who gave me guidance and encouragement on my journey of grief, growth, and transformation, and who supported and challenged my writing. I can't name them all, but those I must acknowledge are professors Arthur Paul Boers, Marlene Kropf, Willard Swartley, June Alliman Yoder, and the professor that for me stands out above the others: Daniel S. Schipani, who advised, inspired, taught, questioned, corrected, encouraged, and nudged me throughout the life-affirming work of my thesis project and pursuit of its publication.

I am very grateful to Herald Press. I thank Levi Miller,

director of Herald Press, for our numerous conversations; Gwen Stamm for designing the cover that is "just right"; and especially Michael Degan, Herald Press book editor, who graciously and skillfully helped transform my academic thesis into a book that maintains integrity but is much more accessible to non-academic readers. I value the gentle but straightforward manner in which Michael responded to my persistent questions and statements to which I held tightly.

In addition, I thank my family for being patient with me during the past three years while I focused extraordinary time and attention on this writing project. Thank you, Mother and siblings, for tolerating me not always taking my turn at hosting family gatherings. Thank you, children: Dori, Carrie, Aaron Jon, and Joel; and daughters-in-law: Nakeisha and Tarah, for putting up with me "always" having my nose in a book or computer and turning down too many invitations to play games or watch movies. I also thank Harold for his love and his belief in me, for the years of our marriage that in some ways prepared me for widowhood, and for his good financial planning that helped make it possible for me to spend time studying and writing.

And most of all, I express deep gratitude, honor, and glory to God, the source of all being, living Word, and Holy Spirit from whom all blessings flow.

Rachel Nafziger Hartzler
Pentecost 2006

Part 1

Grief

—1—

Loss and Suffering

Your joy is your sorrow unmasked.
And the selfsame well from which your laughter rises
was oftentimes filled with your tears.
And how else can it be?
The deeper that sorrow carves into your being,
the more joy you can contain.

When you are joyous, look deep into your heart
and you shall find it is only that which has given you sorrow
that is giving you joy.
When you are sorrowful look again in your heart,
and you shall see that in truth you are weeping for that which
has been your delight.
Some of you say, "Joy is greater than sorrow,"
and others say, "Nay, sorrow is the greater."
But I say unto you, they are inseparable.
—Kahlil Gibran[1]

To live is to suffer loss. Losing is the price we pay for living and for loving. It is imperative that we pay attention to the topic of loss since all will experience it and our lives will be shaped by it. Whenever we love deeply, we become vulnerable to loss. A number of people boldly proclaim that the more hardships one endures, the more one can learn and grow, or that growth cannot occur without some kind of suffering.[2]

Grief is a feeling response to suffering and loss, a response with mental, emotional, physical, and spiritual aspects. Grief results from the loss of a major relationship around which life had been significantly organized. Grief counselor Lyn Prashant writes, "Grief is as universal as the smile."[3]

Loss

Human development might be considered a lifelong series of necessary losses. To grow and develop into separate and responsible people, we must lose and leave and let go.[4] This goes against what we learn from our dominant culture: We grow up. We become educated. We discover our gifts. We find a career. We achieve. We get married. We buy a home. We have children—yes, hopefully they will grow up and leave, but we expect they will come back to visit with grandchildren for us to love and enjoy. This is the American dream. Society tempts us to think that we deserve this, and when anything is taken away from us for which we have worked hard, we scream, "Unfair!"

This American dream does not prepare us for the harsh realities of life. If illness strikes when we have been "successful" and have health insurance, we can find the best medical treatment available. Sometimes the dream can go on. But for most, sooner or later things fall apart. Loved ones die untimely deaths; virginity is violently stolen; divorce divides families; people face financial crises; children die before birth or are born with abnormalities; parents see children suffer failure, loss, or pain. Serious or chronic illness requires some individuals to reorder their lives.

We all deal with varying degrees of loss and tragedy from the moment we are born or, in some circumstances, even before birth. The following categories of loss are adapted from a list created by author Sherill Hostetter:
- Loss of significant people in our lives due to death, divorce, moving, or mental disorder
- Loss of part of ourselves, such as a loss of dreams, job, reputation, or self-esteem

•Losses due to accidents or illness
•Loss of mental acuity, personal abilities, or independence
•Losses due to normal changes such as aging, graduation, and children leaving home
•Loss of what might have been; deprivation due to family dysfunction, abuse, negative choices, infertility, chronic illness of a child, or other painful unchangeable events
•Loss of trust in another person through betrayal or moral failure
•Loss of pets and loss of material objects through fire, theft, or financial crisis[5]

In some cases the "silent" losses, such as loss of self-esteem or loss of trust, are especially difficult, in part because the community does not gather to offer support as it does in the case of death or disaster. All kinds of losses demand attention. Some of the principles elaborated in this book will be pertinent for various types of losses; however, our focus is on the loss of spouses in death.

Loss Is Normal

We live in a culture that would like to ignore suffering and death, and modern medicine has made it possible to diminish physical suffering and delay death. Health and prosperity have become gods for many. Having worked in a healthcare profession for many years, I was committed to health maintenance and illness prevention. Although I loved my work as an obstetrical nurse and childbirth educator, after my husband's death in 1999 I knew it was time for a vocational change. I began seminary studies in 2000, not knowing where I was being led. But on September 11, 2001, my call became clearer. As my teenage daughter, Dori, and I watched with dismay the events unfolding on television in New York, Pennsylvania, and Washington, D.C., that evening, she suggested that I dig out my stethoscope and go work in the hospital again. "That would be a good thing to do," I agreed, "but the work I am doing now is even more important for me."

It's not that I would ignore a crisis in my household or neighborhood. I would lay aside my books and respond if a disaster hit my town. However, I knew I was called to prepare for something else. A number of times during that horrible, unforgettable day, I had remembered words of Ben Ollenburger, AMBS professor of Old Testament, during a class on Isaiah several months earlier. He said that it is crucial in a time of war that we know what we have to say and why we have to say it. It is important to not declare a moratorium on theology, but in a time of war to pursue theology with renewed vigor, dedication, and concentration—just because the potential distractions are so immense.

I knew I needed to learn why and how to talk about the groaning of creation or Rachel weeping for her children. My daughter did not understand; neither would I have understood such a choice at an earlier time in my life.

My priorities changed after my husband's death. Harold had kept his body in good shape by not overeating and by regular vigorous exercise. But he died of a heart attack while jogging, which he did to maintain good cardiovascular function. What irony! I was sure that many who died on September 11 had also practiced good habits for healthy living and had invested wisely for a comfortable retirement. As I am editing this material for publication, we are living in the wake of Hurricane Katrina in the southern United States and in the tremor of a horrific earthquake in Pakistan. Scenes of the Indian Ocean tsunami at Christmastime 2004 are still vivid in our memories. In the 2001 plane crashes, the 2004 tsunami, and the 2005 earthquake, death came with little or no warning. Healthy bodies and retirement dreams turned to ashes, washed away or disappeared in the deadly devastation. Some of the victims had purchased life insurance, but had they prepared to die?

I would not advise anyone to ignore the importance of a healthy lifestyle or to be careless about financial affairs.

But preparing to die is ultimately more significant. Paradoxically, we prepare to die by living. When I graduated from Goshen College in 1970, a group of classmates and I sang a song that was popular at the time. One line went like this: "If I have learned to live, then I have learned to die." How then shall we live? Things with which society lures us—youth and beauty, health and power, admiration and financial success—will not endure. Perhaps living well by being prepared to die is actually counter-cultural.

To live we need to grow. We do have a choice: to live as wounded, empty, slowly dying people, or to find new life. The one way is through depression and defeat; the other way is to be transformed by hope. From the story of Jesus' suffering, death, and resurrection to modern-day stories of suffering and loss, we learn that new life can come from death, that loss and suffering can be the precursor of something new and beautiful. Benedictine nun Joan Chittister says, "Enduring struggle is the price to be paid for becoming everything we are meant to be in the world. . . . The fullness of the self [comes] to birth the only way it really can: in labor and under trial."[6] As we struggle, we move from pain to understanding.

At times it is extremely difficult to choose to grow, but I had grown through two years of mourning my husband's death, and on September 11, I knew I wanted to help people choose to grow and live well. My call from God to some kind of ministry was confirmed. I did not dig out my stethoscope that day. Instead I went to church and prayed with my community of believers.

In the aftermath of September 11, I continued in my struggle to make sense of life and death and God's will and Christian spirituality. I found help in many places—in Scripture and other inspired writings, in worship in various settings, in conversations with many people, in my classes at AMBS. Help for my struggles also came in unexpected places—in front of the Pieta at a Catholic retreat center, on a drive through Masai country in Kenya, and in a café in Berkeley as I conversed with a new friend.

As I read *Scarred by Struggle, Transformed by Hope* by Chittister, I was able to integrate random thoughts and new insights. In our society, so cluttered with diets and exercise clubs, anti-wrinkle creams and age-defying plastic surgery, we lose touch with our deepest longings. As Chittister writes,

> Because we have put too much emphasis on the false perfection of fundamentally imperfect situations, we have overlooked those things in life that are really the ground of our truest strengths: the possibility of conversion, the call to independent thinking, faith in the presence of a companioning God, the courage to persist, surrender to the meanings of the moment, and a sense of limits that leads us to take our proper place in the human race.[7]

Thus cloaked with inspiration from assorted venues and assured of the love of an ever-present God, I continued my journey of finding my "proper place in the human race."

Loss of a Loved One in Death

We can never totally prepare for the death of a loved one. Even when death is expected, the bereaved talk about a sense of shock when the end comes, a sense of not anticipating the emotional chaos, which may include relief, guilt, fear, despair, anger, and intense sadness all at the same time. We know that countless millions have coped with the loss of loved ones, and yet the circumstances and experiences of each person's loss are unique and often shocking.

There are typically some differences in the pattern of grief in the early weeks and months following the *sudden* death of a loved one as compared to a death that is *anticipated* following an illness. Gale Livengood compares the difference between sudden death and anticipated death as the difference between a tornado and a hurricane.[8] With a tornado there is little or no warning of the destruction to come; with a hurricane come warnings and the option to prepare. But both create a trail of devastation and loss. Similarly, the differences between mourning sudden deaths and anticipated deaths are not as great after the initial period. In fact, after the first year the differences often are insignificant.

In addition, each person's loss and suffering is unique, and one person's suffering cannot be compared to another's. In *Man's Search for Meaning*, Viktor Frankl, who himself survived concentration camps during World War II, graphically describes how, although the intensity of suffering varies, suffering relatively minor losses can consume a person just as the most vicious or violent suffering does.

> A [person's] suffering is similar to the behavior of gas. If a certain quantity of gas is pumped into an empty chamber, it will fill the chamber completely and evenly, no matter how big the chamber. Thus suffering completely fills the human soul and conscious mind, no matter whether the suffering is great or little. Therefore the "size" of human suffering is absolutely relative.[9]

Yet, suffering the loss of a loved one in death is the greatest suffering many people endure.

People are changed by the death of a beloved person. We cannot hover around life-and-death issues without being changed. The death of a spouse is a unique crisis but it is not necessarily the worst kind of loss. Elsie Neufeld makes insightful observations about the grief caused by the death of parent, spouse, child, and sibling: With the death of a parent, we are partially severed from our past; with the death of a spouse we are cut off in some ways from our present life; and the death of a child interrupts our dreams for the future. However, in certain profound ways the death of a sibling disrupts our connections with past, present, *and* future.[10] So, while a sibling death may not be "worse" than other deaths, it may be more encompassing.

Researchers Holmes and Masuda reported in 1973 that the death of a spouse is the most severe stressor that a person can experience. They placed the death of a spouse above the death of a child or other family member. [11]

However, during the past years I have asked numerous people who have lost both a spouse and a child in death which was the most difficult, and in most cases, the death of a child was described as worse.

One woman whose husband and son were killed together in a plane crash reported that her grief was so immense that for a long time she could not identify which individual she was mourning at any given time. When the day finally came that she could mourn for them individually, it was the death of her son that was the most painful. Another woman whose husband and child had both died explained it this way:

There was no difference in the pain. I hurt so badly in both cases I thought I would go blind. I could not tell that one hurt more than the other. The difference was the grief following the death of my husband was a slow process of turning loose—of saying goodbye. The grief following the death of my child was a process of hanging on—of trying not to say goodbye. There was a sense that the child had not lived long enough to establish significance and I needed to establish significance for the child. I need to walk through the world for the child.[12]

Professor and veteran counselor Wayne Oates confirmed my suspicion that Holmes and Masuda's conclusions are not necessarily valid. First, he writes that the study's population was only hospitalized patients. Second, he has found in his own work that the death of a child seems to be the most devastating experience families encounter.[13] Peg Elliott Mayo describes the death of a child as wrenching a "parent's soul harder than any other personal catastrophe."[14]

In addition to the deaths of grandparents during my youth, I have suffered the deaths of my father, my husband, a sister-in-law, and a beloved nephew. Cousins and dear friends have also died. Of these, the death that has affected me most significantly is that of my husband. However, if one of my children dies before I do, I suspect that that death will affect me even more profoundly.

Along with various tumultuous feelings, questions about life and death emerge for most people who have lost a loved one, especially if the death was untimely. Some people don't want to go on living themselves. An important work that has served as an essential resource for my study is James Loder's *The Logic of the Spirit*. He offers insightful interpretations of how God's Spirit interacts with the human spirit and how human development is affected by that interaction. Loder poses two questions at the onset of this interdisciplinary work: "What is a lifetime?" and "Why do I live it?" After offering insightful paradigms of human growth and spiritual formation, he suggests an answer near the end of the book: "My life is an incomplete act of God's immense love toward God's creation; it is an act that is completed only as I return with my lifetime that same love to God and to God's creation. . . . Love precedes meaning and purpose and is the substance of their power to shape and direct a lifetime."[15] These ideas integrate love and loss, formation and transformation, and have the potential of guiding one on a journey of inner discovery.

Loss of a Spouse in Death

"What is 'one flesh' when it is separated by death?" asked one widow who responded to the questionnaire I distributed. She wondered why God's plan "calls for this." Harold's death caused deeper pain, more wrenching of my inner being, and a bigger void than I could have imagined. It was an unexpected, unwilled dissolution of my marriage. How can a person be married one minute and not the next?

Some individuals feel isolated in their anguish and ashamed of what they are feeling. From the beginning, I was surrounded by widowed people and read books by and about others whose spouses had died, and I was comforted to know I was not alone in my feelings. Some gave words to feelings that felt inexpressible. C. S. Lewis referred to the death of his wife as an amputation, but one in which the same leg is cut off time and time again.[16] He asked, "How often will the vast emptiness astonish me like a complete novelty and make me say, 'I never realized my loss till this moment'? . . . The first plunge of the knife into the flesh is felt again and again."[17]

Doris Moreland Jones calls spousal death an amputation without anesthesia.[18] Others have described the death of husband or wife as a tearing or gouging out of the heart or as becoming a "half self." Spousal bereavement is a painful and unsettling process that affects most, if not all, areas of a widowed person's life. For most people, being widowed is the most disruptive and challenging experience they will ever face. The pain is unimaginable; only by experiencing it can one know this pain.

Prashant has studied physical pain in relation to grief. She defines grief as "a mental and emotional experience, usually triggered by a traumatic loss that has physiological correlates associated with deep pain." She thinks that grief often creates "long-lasting physical imbalances in the human body" due in part to our culture's ineffective responses to grieving people.

To address this concern, Prashant has developed a program for working with grieving people, which she practices and about which she writes and teaches. To describe this process, she has coined the term *degriefing*, which she defines as "the process of recognizing mental and physical pain which accompanies grief, and treating it with a combination of somatic therapies." Degriefing is used "to unlock and remove grief from an individual's body, and thereby heal not only physical symptoms, but mental and emotional wounds as well."[19]

I discovered Prashant and her writings when I was well along in my grief journey. Earlier, about a year after Harold's death, I had been crying out to God, wondering why the death of a spouse is such a painful and difficult ordeal. After all, people had been surviving this type of loss throughout the ages. What I finally recognized is that, just as there is mystery in the way two become one when sexually united in marriage, so there is mystery in the depth of the pain that occurs when "one of the one" dies. How does the one become two again, so one can go on living when the other has died? Naming sexuality and death as mystery helps me to accept the paradoxes and ambiguities that accompany the death of a spouse.

Acknowledging the painful dimensions of separation in death as a mystery did not resolve all my questions. Yet I can live with mystery, and as I do, I continue to ask questions, not feverishly, but in a mode of waiting until I am ready to accept more truth.

The Living Well After the Death of a Spouse Questionnaire

I was ready for more truth when I designed the questionnaire I sent to 220 people who are widowed or were at one time. In an effort to allow people to feel comfortable enough to give honest answers, I committed to treating the information confidentially and arranged for the responses to be returned anonymously.

One hundred five women and forty-five men responded, along with two respondents who did not indicate gender.[20] Their ages at the time of the spouse's death ranged from under forty to over eighty years. Respondents included those widowed less than a year to more than twenty years.

Demographic data from Living Well questionnaire received January through March 2004

152 respondents
   105 women (69% of total)
   45 men (30%)
   2 of unidentified gender

Of the 105 women:
   11 women were under 40 when widowed
   22 were between ages 40 and 49 when widowed
   26 were between 50 and 59 when widowed
   24 were between 60 and 69 when widowed
   17 were between 70 and 79 when widowed
   3 were over 80 when widowed
   (2 women did not indicate their ages when widowed)

continued on next page

Of the 45 men:
   8 men were under 40 when widowed
   7 were between ages 40 and 49 when widowed
   5 were between 50 and 59 when widowed
   12 were between 60 and 69 when widowed
   10 were between 70 and 79 when widowed
   2 were over 80 when widowed
   (1 man did not indicate his age when widowed.)

Length of time since spouse died:
   1 man and 10 women had been widowed within the previous year
   4 men and 8 women had been widowed between 1 and 2 years earlier
   2 men and 11 women (and one unknown gender) had been widowed between 2 and 3 years
   2 men and 14 women had been widowed between 3 and 4 years earlier
   4 men and 4 women had been widowed between 4 and 5 years earlier
   15 men and 19 women (and one unknown gender) had been widowed between 5 and 10 years
   7 men and 28 women had been widowed between 10 and 20 years earlier
   9 men and 11 women had been widowed more than 20 years earlier

Church Affiliation:
   Of the 152 respondents, 113 stated they were Mennonite (74%), 7 were nondenominational, 4 Methodist, 3 Brethren, 3 Presbyterian, 3 Catholics, and 2 Missionary Church, plus 1 each from Church of the Brethren, Baptist, Church of God, Quaker, and Religious Science.
   Ten did not state their church affiliation and one indicated no church affiliation.

I have learned much from those who so graciously entrusted me with their stories. Some people articulated things that I had found difficult to put into words. My mind was stretched in new ways. Many of the theories I had formulated about grief were confirmed. An extra bonus for me was learning that I am "normal" (or at least typical) in most of my responses to Harold's death. If reading responses and summaries in this book helps to normalize grief for others, I will be grateful.

Most Difficult Tasks

Although the focus of my study was not on the early months following the death of a spouse, I asked a few such questions to help establish a beginning point. The list of "most difficult tasks" named some of the ways in a spouse's death is uniquely complicated.

According to 30 percent of my respondents, finances and business were the most challenging things to deal with in the first few months after being widowed. Taking care of the car(s) was mentioned by a number of women. Respondents said making decisions regarding a business was one of the most difficult tasks. Although a few named specific decisions, for most it was any kind of decision. One added that just thinking was difficult.

Second were parenting issues, ranging from childcare to putting children to bed alone to dealing with teenagers. Twenty-two percent named this, confessing that it was extremely demanding to help their children grieve when they were overwhelmed with grief themselves. The questionnaire didn't ask about the ages of children when first widowed, but I suspect that, of those who did have children at home, nearly all would say that parenting alone was challenging and at times grueling.

Dealing with loneliness or "adjusting to being alone" was the third most difficult task, according to the respondents. Many were specific about the difficulty of daily events. Eating alone was one of the hardest, as was going to bed alone. Many said that going to social events without their spouse was difficult. One replied that coming home alone from social events was a most difficult task.

Pastor and author Eugene Peterson says that the most horrible things about loss and pain are the loneliness and the rejection that accompany suffering.[21] To some extent, each person must suffer his or her own loss and must struggle with his or her own dilemma. The suffering usually cannot be taken away, and seldom can someone else suffer in the place of a victim. Even those who feel God's presence and who are surrounded by others at some level suffer alone. As Henri Nouwen wrote, "Isolation is among the worst of human sufferings."[22] For widowed people the loss of spouse is compounded by isolation because, for many of us, the person who could best offer comfort in our sorrow is the very person who has died.

Going to church was the fourth most difficult task during those early months of loss (16 percent of the respondents). Numerous people mentioned that going to church without the deceased spouse continued to be tough. However, it is noteworthy that people continued going. One stated that although it was very difficult, it was one of the most important things she did.

It is reasonable that being in the place where God is named and God's presence is acknowledged stirs deep emotions. During worship, the Spirit of God, which is deep within all who have been created in the image of God, connects with our human spirits. It is also deep within that the intense pain of loss is felt. The space where we meet God and the space where we feel emotional pain are mysteriously interwoven. I struggled with going to church for many weeks, but I went because I felt a great need to be within my community of praying people, partly because it was very challenging for me to pray. During those early months, words often wouldn't come when I attempted to address God.

Singing in church and music in general can bring tears to a grieving person. This does not mean that it is terribly difficult to sing or to listen to music, but rather that music evokes intense feelings. Music acts as a medium through which many people go beyond themselves and are connected with the transcendent. In addition, couples who worship together may find that a profound spiritual intimacy with each other occurs when they sing and pray side by side.

Thus the losses that are experienced in worship when a loved one has died can be multilayered.

Taking care of the clothing and other personal possessions of the deceased spouse also can be difficult. One woman said that she did it gradually as she felt up to it. Another added that even though she did it on her own timetable, it was still difficult. Some told me stories of being pressured to get rid of things quickly and later regretting that they had done so. Only the widowed person knows when it is the right time. Keeping and treasuring pieces of clothing or other memorabilia indefinitely is normal; it is not a sign of denial.

Feeling overwhelmed, feeling numb, lacking energy and motivation, feeling fatigue and exhaustion, and having difficulty focusing were also common during those early weeks and months. One respondent said that getting up in the morning was the most difficult task. Fatigue is very common among those in mourning; the work of grief is enormously exhausting. Some feel consumed by grief and others are rendered nearly helpless by the heavy burden that often accompanies it.

Panic attacks may occur during this period, and a few wrote that they wanted to die also. These are all normal responses to loss. Grief's physical symptoms (known as the somatic effects of grief) are often confused with the symptoms of clinical depression. Grief and depression are not the same thing, even though depression may include grieving and grief can trigger depression. Psychiatrist and grief counselor Otto Klassen defines clinical depression as a pathologic state of mind, meaning a chemical imbalance in the brain. Mild *feelings* of depression are typical for a person in grief and do not necessarily need medical treatment. Feelings of depression associated with grief should be listened to and attended to but usually these feelings will eventually lift without medical intervention.

For some people, the dailyness of grief was most wearisome. Simply doing the tasks of daily living was challenging. One person said that daily tasks were more difficult than holidays. Another wrote, "Taking out the garbage—I have no idea why!" I have an idea. I seldom took out the garbage when Harold was living. Our garbage pickup at the street was on Monday mornings, so on Sunday evenings, usually after dark, Harold took the garbage cans to the street. For many weeks I cried every Sunday evening when I did the garbage chore, being acutely aware of his absence at those times. After a few months I remembered that he had often called me outside to look at the stars after he had done that routine task. So I began to pause and look at the stars (when they were visible in the Indiana sky) before going back into the house. Eventually that mundane chore was transformed for me into a time of looking up, remembering Harold, and thinking about heaven and Creator God.

Housework, household chores, home repairs, and home maintenance also showed up on the list of most difficult tasks. Some widowed people were in situations in which they had to move. Several mentioned moving as difficult, another named finding a job, and others mentioned going back to work.

Finding a new identity was a most difficult task as well.[23] One thoughtful respondent said the most difficult part was "taking back what my spouse 'held' for me, e.g. emotional support, understanding and other things of an intangible but supportive nature."

One individual summed up her feelings in one word: "Everything!" The list of difficult tasks seems to go on and on. For most people everything, or almost everything, is difficult to do after the death of a spouse.

I had invested more in my relationship with Harold than in any relationship I've ever had. I've also invested a lot in my children, although that investment is much different. I give my time and energy, make sacrifices, and carry my children in my heart so that they will grow up and become healthy individuals, ready to make their own marks on the world.

Investment with a spouse is more profound than that

with a child. In the intercourse of daily activities as well as in sexual intercourse, we learn to know and become known by our spouses. That knowing and becoming vulnerable connects us in deeper ways than with any other humans. The mother-child relationship is deep and significant, but it lacks the reciprocity present in a good marriage.

Breaking deep bonds causes pain and suffering. The point is not to try to evaluate whether one kind of suffering is worse than another, but to acknowledge that suffering does occur when a loved one dies and that the suffering following the death of spouse, lover, and/or life companion is unique.

Suffering

Is there a purpose in suffering? Some claim there is. Frankl said, "If there is a meaning in life at all, then there must be a meaning in suffering. Suffering is an ineradicable part of life. . . . Without suffering and death, human life cannot be complete."[24] Twentieth-century Christian theologians such as Karl Barth, Dietrich Bonhoeffer, and Jürgen Moltmann have explored the meaning of the experience of suffering.

Suffering as a Biblical and Christian Theme

As Christians, we worship a God who suffers. We often long for a God who prevents suffering, but instead God comes in love and is present with us in our suffering and pain. And not only that, God helps us find meaning in our suffering and leads us toward transformation to something richer and more meaningful.

In the biblical epic

The Bible holds many accounts of suffering, anguish, and distress. Applicable to our discussion is the story of Jacob who wrestled with God. When we live within the paradoxes of life and ask our questions, we are also wrestling with God. From Jacob to Job to Jeremiah to the psalmists, confronting God is part of the biblical tradition.

Jewish philosopher Abraham Heschel says that "the refusal to accept the harshness of God's ways in the name of God's love [is] . . . an authentic form of prayer."[25] This kind of refusal or declaration to God is wrestling in prayer.

Jacob was given the name *Israel*, which means God-Wrestler. As Christians we sometimes call ourselves the new Israel—new God-Wrestlers. When we confront or wrestle with God, we are interacting with God and are thereby close to God. When we have a relationship with God, it is appropriate to engage in wrestling. Don Postema writes,

> God is our lover. But we struggle with the divine lover just as we struggle with our human lovers. Because we know there's a basis of trust beneath our differences and disagreements and disappointments, we're able to argue with those we love as well as relate warmly to them. . . . Surprisingly, our angry words can be a way of coming back to God rather than distancing ourselves from God. The wrestle may be like a violent embrace. And once we wrestle, we may go back into life, limping but renewed—like Jacob, physically lame but spiritually regenerated.[26]

A striking poetic rendition of the Jacob story is "Come, O Thou Traveler Unknown," by Charles Wesley. Many meaningful descriptions in his poem connect the story of Jacob to our stories.

> My strength is gone, my nature dies. . . . I fall, and yet by faith I stand. . . .
> What though my shrinking flesh complain, and murmur to contend so long,
> I rise superior to my pain; when I am weak then I am strong. . . .
> Lame as I am, I take the prey, hell, earth, and sin with ease overcome.
> I leap for joy, pursue my way, and as a bounding hart fly home,
> Through all eternity to prove thy nature, and thy name is Love.[27]

Although knowing God's love is reassuring, questions about struggling and suffering remain. In his novel *Gates of the Forest*, Elie Wiesel gives one of his characters these words: "The Talmud tells us that God suffers with man. Why? In order to strengthen the bonds between creation and Creator; God chooses to suffer in order to better understand man and be better understood by him."[28] My grief journey took a positive turn when I finally realized not only that was God *present* with me in my grief, but also that God suffered with me.

The faithfulness of God throughout the Old Testament is important to Jews and Christians alike. However, for Christians, understanding suffering in light of Jesus is critical.

In light of the life, suffering, and death of Jesus

The passion of Jesus—his suffering and death—was a big topic of conversation during 2004 as Mel Gibson's film *The Passion of the Christ* hit theaters across North America and beyond. Through this dramatic portrayal of Jesus' passion in his final hours before his crucifixion, millions of Christians and non-Christians were drawn into thinking about this momentous, earth-shaking event. For Christians Jesus' death was the great reversal of history. At-one-ment with God became possible without the offering of sacrifices for sins. In the death of Jesus, reconciliation with God was made possible for all humanity.

Christianity embraces the Paschal mystery, the movement from death to life through the life, crucifixion, death, and resurrection of Jesus Christ. Although this mystery has been acknowledged and proclaimed in Roman Catholic spirituality for centuries, all are invited to enter this mystery, to participate in the natural rhythm of death and resurrection as a lifelong spiritual rhythm. In our addicted, death-avoiding, and death-denying culture, the Paschal mystery is not attractive. But it seems as though spiritual growth may not occur without some kind of death—without encounters of loss and suffering.

Both Ronald Rolheiser, a Catholic, and Jean Stairs, a Protestant, offer insights into this mystery.[29] "Recognizing death as part of the daily rhythm of life helps us to live as authentic spiritual beings," writes Stairs.[30] Discovering that there is often *death in life* opens one to understand that there is *life in death* in addition to *life beyond death*. This mystery is most poignantly illustrated in the death and resurrection of Jesus. In his life he made the reign of God visible and in his death he overcame the forces of evil that resist God's rule.

Although many people throughout time have suffered greatly, no one but Jesus has known the true essence and the total breadth, depth, and darkness of human misery. The great twentieth-century theologian Karl Barth declared, "What we see and note and know and more or less painfully experience of [human misery] is only the shadow of his cross touching us." He pointed to both the paradox and the mystery in suffering. When his own son died, Barth used for his funeral sermon the text from 1 Corinthians 13:12: "For now we see in a mirror, dimly, but then we will see face to face." Because of God's grace extended through the death and resurrection of Jesus Christ, light does shine in the darkness and "we doubt and nevertheless are confident, . . . we cry and nevertheless are joyful."[31] God chooses to be vulnerable as God invites people to relate as free subjects to and active partners with God. Creator God suffered when Jesus suffered. In this way God joins in the suffering of all humanity.

Out of an understanding of God's suffering love, theologian Jürgen Moltmann promotes a Christ-centered theology of hope. He writes, "Basically, every Christian theology is consciously or unconsciously answering the question, 'Why have you forsaken me?'" He claims that a theology of the cross goes beyond understanding suffering, saying, "The God-forsaken cry with which Christ dies on the cross [is] the criterion for all theology which claims to be Christian." Moltmann's concern with the phenomenon of hope is rooted in his experiences as a prisoner of war. He found hope as he read the psalms of lament and reflected on Jesus' cry from the cross, knowing that he was not alone. He recognized that Jesus took all who suffer with him on his way to resurrection. He then "began to summon up the courage to live again, seized by a great hope."[32] This hope that grows out of lament is featured throughout this book.

God's power is demonstrated in the cross and resurrection of Jesus. But in the cross do we find a God who is not all-powerful? Dietrich Bonhoeffer said yes, claiming that God chose to become "weak and powerless in the world, and that is exactly the way, the only way, in which [God] can be with us." Instead of a powerful God who removes suffering, Jesus showed us a God who helps us in our weakness and suffering. In the same way that Jesus invited his disciples to pray with him in the garden of Gethsemane, so are we "challenged to participate in the sufferings of God at the hands of a godless world."[33] However, more questions beg for attention.

The Question of Theodicy

The question of whether God allows suffering has been asked throughout the ages, from Job of Uz to present-day ordinary people. Rabbi Harold Kushner says that nearly every meaningful conversation he has had about God and religion has either started with the question of why the righteous suffer or soon moves to it.[34]

The question of theodicy, humanity's attempt to reconcile this apparent contradiction between the experience of suffering and the existence of a loving and powerful God, is one I have spent much time pondering during the past several years. It would be easier to understand evil if we believed God to be good but not powerful, or if we believed God to be powerful but not good. One of my seminary professors, Perry Yoder, asked variations of this perennial question: How do we put together trust and faith in God with the fact of what really did and does happen? Do the promises of God sometimes fail? What is the responsibility on the part of the people?

I ask these questions anew time and time again, when

loved ones die, especially promising young people, and when people die in unnecessary and futile wars. Even bigger questions erupt when tsunamis, hurricanes, and earthquakes wreak horrendous devastation. Some people fail to ask these questions, thinking that whatever happens is God's will. I believe that because we are human, we must ask questions and wrestle with God.

The Hebrew understanding of God includes the notion that God causes everything that comes to pass, both the good and the bad. This insight is helpful for those who wonder about some Old Testament descriptions of God's involvement in catastrophic events. Contemporary understandings of evil in the world offer different perspectives. Willard Swartley gives a present-day Anabaptist perspective in his list of theses that describe a biblical theology of healing. Three of his seven theses are helpful in dealing with the question of theodicy:

- God is God, and we are weak, mortal, frail creatures.
- Illness puts us in a quandary before God, because it interrupts and challenges our experience of God's good world.
- In our suffering God is not absent but is present in love.[35]

Among the numerous books I have read, four monographs stand out as stories that point to some answers for the question of theodicy: *When Bad Things Happen to Good People* by Harold Kushner, *A Grief Observed* by C. S. Lewis, *A Grace Disguised: How the Soul Grows Through Loss* by Gerald Sittser,[36] and *Lament for a Son* by Nicholas Wolterstorff.[37] Lewis and Sittser were both widowed, and Kushner and Wolterstorff both had young sons who died. These four each wrote as wounded theologians, telling about their immeasurable grief, their struggles with God, and the answers that finally came.

Kushner, a rabbi, believes that the only question that really matters is why bad things happen to good people. He weaves the story of his struggle with his son's dying into an excellent and profound treatise. He comes to find the answer to his question in relationship to God, the God who does not send problems, but who gives strength to cope with them. More important than figuring out the source of tragedy or suffering is asking where the experience of it leads. Kushner concludes with the bold statement that perhaps we need to forgive God for making a less-than-perfect world.[38]

In a car crash caused by a drunk driver, Sittser's wife, his mother, and one of his four children were killed. Through this staggering, catastrophic loss, Sittser came to know God's grace in powerful ways. He lost the world that he loved, but he gained a deeper awareness of grace, grace that helped him to see more clearly his purpose in life and to value life more than ever. He experienced personal transformation and came to understand that transformation comes only through grace.

Sittser struggled with the terror of randomness. He asked, "Why me?" but then needed to also ask, "Why *not* me?" He recognized that living in a world with grace was far better than living in a world of absolute fairness: "A world with grace will give us even more than we deserve. It will give us life, even in our suffering."[39]

A significant difference between Sittser and Kushner is that Sittser is Christian, and for him the resurrection of Jesus plays a vital role in understanding suffering. Life, not death, has the final word.

> We doubt, yet try to believe; we suffer, yet long for real healing; we inch hesitantly toward death, yet see death as the door to resurrection. This ambivalence of the soul reveals the dual nature of life. We are creatures made of dust; yet we know that we were made for something more. A sense of eternity resides in our hearts. Living with this ambivalence is both difficult and vital. It stretches our souls, challenging us to acknowledge our mortality and yet to continue to hope for final victory—victory Jesus won for us in his death and resurrection.[40]

Wolterstorff's Lament for a Son is reminiscent of Sittser's A Grace Disguised (and vice versa) in that they ask many of the same theological questions and find hope in their Christian faith. However, Lament for a Son is much shorter, more succinct, and more poetic.

In her classic book, *Suffering*, Dorothee Soelle asks who will work to change conditions that lead to suffering. It certainly cannot be those who are incapable of suffering or who have lost the ability to perceive the suffering of others. "Neither is it those who are so thoroughly destroyed through continual suffering that they can respond only in helpless or aggressive attempts to flee," Soelle writes. She then boldly asserts that only those who themselves suffer will do the hard work of attempting to abolish conditions under which people are exposed to senseless, unnecessary suffering, such as hunger, oppression, or torture.[41] I would include war and other types of violence and abuse. In such situations, many people have endured suffering and then diligently participated in efforts to eliminate it.

Nevertheless, the answers to *why* bad things happen remain unclear. There are no simple explanations that are satisfying. We need to wrestle with God when atrocious things happen that it seems God could have prevented; but eventually, like Job, we can come to find God's presence more comforting than any answers.

After Harold's death, I came to depend on God more than ever. But would a loving God set up that tragedy in my life so that I would draw near? I don't think so. My understanding of God is that God loves friends *and* enemies, sends rain on the just and on the unjust, and overcomes evil through self-sacrificing love rather than through violent retribution. In addition, God wants us to *choose* to be in relationship. We are *invited* into covenant with God.

AMBS graduate Myrna Miller uses a beautiful metaphor to describe God as paradoxically both transcendent and immanent.

> This is a God who is responsive to our needs, who is aware of every nuance of our feelings. This is a God who leads us in the dance, gracefully assisting our steps, steadying us, leading us into complex steps we couldn't

have learned on our own. This is a God who knows we'll get off balance . . . but who lovingly and patiently pulls us back into the dance.[42]

Wolterstorff points to the great mystery: "To redeem our brokenness and lovelessness the God who suffers with us did not strike some mighty blow of power, but sent his beloved son to suffer like us, through his suffering to redeem us from suffering and evil. Instead of explaining our suffering, God shares it."[43] Herein lies great hope!

I choose to live with the question of theodicy at this time in this way: There is mystery in God's ways. We may need to struggle and ask why until we discover that we can live without answers. So although it is important to wrestle with the question of theodicy, the time comes when by grace we are enabled to lay it aside and with God's help to live fully in the present, while at the same time moving on to other questions and concerns.

Suffering and Joy

When we enter into grief and "drink the cup of sorrow," new discoveries will be made, as Nouwen notes.

> In the midst of the sorrows is consolation, in the midst of the darkness is light, in the midst of the despair is hope, in the midst of Babylon is a glimpse of Jerusalem, and in the midst of the army of demons is the consoling angel. The cup of sorrow, inconceivable as it seems, is also the cup of joy![44]

This statement startled me when I came across it early in my grief journey. At first I doubted that it could be true, but as I lived with the idea, I slowly absorbed its truth. When a bereaved person discovers this awesome truth, life takes on new meaning, and continuing along the journey becomes less difficult. Nouwen encourages reflection about sorrow and joy:

> The cup of life is the cup of joy as much as it is the cup of sorrow. It is the cup in which sorrows and joys, sadness and gladness, mourning and dancing are never separated. If joys could not be where sorrows are, the cup of life would never be drinkable. That is why we have to

hold the cup in our hands and look carefully to see the joys hidden in our sorrows.[45]

There is an old saying, "When the heart weeps for what it has lost, the spirit laughs for what it has found." It is a paradox that pathos and joy coexist in the midst of suffering. And yet that is a lesson waiting to be learned. Joy and sorrow are no more mutually exclusive than winter and sunlight. Kahlil Gibran wrote, "Your joy is your sorrow unmasked."[46] Marlene Kropf and Eddy Hall explain in *Praying with the Anabaptists* that "the secret to joy in suffering . . . is not in denying the pain, but in focusing on . . . God's great love and care for us. . . . When we feel intensely loved in the midst of our suffering, suffering cannot take our joy away."[47] Thus, while drinking a cup of sorrow in God's presence, we can begin to taste a bit of joy.

Many spiritual writers throughout the ages have explained the connectedness of suffering and joy. Catholic priest and renowned spiritual director Richard Rohr says we cannot experience deep joy without knowing sorrow.

Dietrich Bonhoeffer expanded on this idea in his poem "Sorrow and Joy," saying both are "imperturbable, mighty, ruinous and compelling," transfiguring those they encounter, "investing them with strange gravity and a spirit of worship." He said, "Joy is rich in fears; sorrow has its sweetness. Undistinguishable from each other they approach us from eternity, equally potent in their power and terror."[48]

To appreciate the value of something, we must experience what it is like to be without it. One woman said, "I didn't know the depth of love I had for my spouse until after he died." Eugene Herr talks about appreciating the "is-ness" of life—celebrating what *is*.[49] Perhaps this is a spiritual discipline that must be cultivated. Young people may be unable to understand the "is-ness" of life until they have experienced or at least observed some kind of deprivation. However, the young Gibran wrote,

I would not exchange the sorrows of my heart for the joys of the multitude. And I would not have the tears that sadness makes to flow from my every part turn into laughter.

I would that my life remain a tear and a smile. A tear to purify my heart and give me understanding of life's secrets and hidden things. . . . A tear to unite me with those of broken heart; a smile to be a sign of my joy in existence.[50]

Similarly, Nouwen wrote,

Mortification—literally "making death"—is what life is all about, a slow discovery of the mortality of all that is created so that we can appreciate its beauty without clinging to it as if it were a lasting possession. Our lives can indeed be seen as a process of becoming familiar with death, as a school in the art of dying. . . . When we see life constantly relativized by death, we can enjoy it for what it is: a free gift. . . . In every arrival there is a leave-taking; in each one's growing up there is a growing old; in every smile there is a tear; and in every success there is a loss. All living is dying and all celebration is mortification too.[51]

Suffering opens possibilities for greater joy. Tears of sorrow purify the heart so that it can be filled with joy. What mystery!

Living with Suffering

The grief I felt following Harold's death plunged me into the depths of my being, depths I had not known existed. In *Lament for a Son*, Wolterstorff writes of experiencing something similar: "Out of my self I traveled on a journey of love and attached this self of mine to Eric, my son. Now he's gone, lost, ripped loose from love, and the ache of loss sinks down, and down, deep down into my soul, deep beyond all telling. How deep do souls go?"[52]

In this new terrain, there is much to be learned. The challenge is to find the courage to endure, to stay with the suffering long enough so growth and transformation can begin to occur.

Enduring with hope

Can one endure suffering when there is no hope? The answer seems to be no. In *The Wounded Healer*, Nouwen wrote,

A man can keep his sanity and stay alive as long as there is at least one person who is waiting for him. The mind of man can indeed rule his body even when there is little health left. A dying mother can stay alive to see her son before she gives up the struggle; a soldier can prevent his mental and physical disintegration when he knows that his wife and children are waiting for him. But when "nothing and nobody" is waiting, there is no chance to survive in the struggle for life.[53]

Likewise, in his story of fellow Jews in concentration camps during the Holocaust, Frankl says that those who survived did so because they had something to live for—something beyond themselves. He tells of two prisoners who contemplated suicide because "they had nothing more to expect from life. In both cases it was a matter of getting them to realize that life was still expecting something from them." One had a child waiting for him; the other had unfinished writing projects.

[The] uniqueness which distinguishes each individual and gives a meaning to his existence has a bearing on the creative work as much as it does on human love. . . . A [person] who becomes conscious of the responsibility he bears toward a human being who affectionately waits for him, or to an unfinished work, will never be able to throw away his life. He knows the "why" for his existence, and will be able to bear almost any "how."[54]

These are stories of hope found in the struggle. The apostle Paul said in Romans 5:3-4 that "suffering produces endurance, and endurance produces character, and character produces hope." So is hope a by-product of suffering? Chittister says it is, stating that hope and struggle are "of a piece. . . . Hope is built into struggle."[55]

But endurance cannot be bypassed. It is a critical step between suffering and hope. Although it is really part of the suffering, endurance is the way we can choose to live with suffering.

Endurance is about having heart enough to keep on trying to do the possible even if it is unattainable. . . . Endurance does not mean "success." It means being willing to cope with what is. . . . Endurance is not misery, not martyrdom, not spiritual machoism. Endurance means that I intend to survive the worst, singing as I go, knowing as Jacob did, that "I have seen the face of God and survived." . . . Endurance is not negation of life; it is commitment to whatever makes life worthwhile. . . . It allows us to be committed and realistic at the same time. . . . Endurance is the sacrament of commitment.[56]

At the end of Jacob's struggle with God, he was blessed for enduring the struggle, not for winning it. Enduring means living in the present. Although we need to tell our stories and find ways to reconcile the past, we need to live in and learn from the present. It is only when we are in the present that we can look to the future with hope and move forward. Saint Thérèse of Lisieux, who endured a chronic illness that led to her death, wrote in her journal, "When we yield to discouragement it is usually because we give too much thought to the past and to the future."[57] As we suffer and struggle, enduring the present with hope, we will discover we are growing.

Growing in suffering

To live is to suffer loss. Suffering is part of the human experience. Some suggest that it is only through our suffering that we grow. I resisted that idea when I first read it—not questioning that growth could be a result of suffering, but that suffering might be the only way to grow. Is there really no easy way to grow? Would it not be possible to grow as we prosper, in good health and surrounded by loved ones whose behavior is always pleasant?

From a psychological perspective, Prashant says, "Grief is the most available resource for personal transformation." There is a choice, but to choose not to grow is to miss an opportunity. She also says that "if we choose to deny or ignore our grief, or fail to convert or transform it, we are missing a cultural opportunity to enrich and enlighten our social existence. We possess [grief] as the most available . . . emotional commodity to exchange through conversion."[58] More specifically, a journey in grief is a profound opportunity for spiritual growth, for the human spirit to connect with the Divine Spirit.

Many kinds of growth and even gifts can come from suffering. Reflecting on the book of Lamentations, Eugene Peterson said, "Prayer is suffering's best result."[59] So we move from loss and suffering to prayer, where the suffering person most often comes crying out with laments.

—2—

Lament: Responding to Loss and Suffering

Nevertheless I am continually with you;
you hold my right hand.
—Psalm 73:23[1]

For it is in listening to the music of the past
that I can sing in the present
and dance into the future.
—Alan Wolfelt[2]

Suffering comes to all and it comes unbidden. It is passive, passed out to us, usually related to situations beyond our control. Struggling, on the other hand, is active; it is a response to suffering. The essence of struggle is choosing life, deciding to allow something new to happen.[3] Struggling is accepting the invitation to transformation.

I propose that lament is the paradigm within which struggling can best take place. People who suffer and feel grief must find ways to lament—to acknowledge to themselves and to express to God the pain of the loss—before they can move along on a healing journey. Additionally, for people who experience great loss to remain comfortable in their social settings, they must go through some kind of corporate lament. Both private and corporate lament are crucial. We will consider some of the dynamics of private lament here and address corporate lament in chapter 5.

The Necessity of Lament

Lamenting is crying out in pain, wailing in sorrow, allowing suffering to come to voice, uttering complaints to God. It is a powerful, psychologically cathartic experience. Psychologists, philosophers, theologians, and pastoral care providers concur that expressing grief is a necessary response to significant loss. Even public officials and politicians agree that after events like those that occurred on September 11, we need to gather together in some way and speak about the horrors.

As life goes on, we face more and more losses. Author Ronald Rolheiser, a Catholic priest, suggests that the greatest spiritual and psychological challenge for adults after midlife is mourning our losses and deaths: "Unless we mourn properly our hurts, our losses, life's unfairness, our shattered dreams, our radical inconsummation, and all the life that we once had but that has now passed us by, we will live in either an unhealthy fantasy or an ever-intensifying bitterness."[4]

The psychological term for expressing grief is *mourning*. In popular literature and in conversation, most people use the words *grief* and *mourning* interchangeably. However, Alan Wolfelt makes a helpful distinction between them. He defines *grief* as the "collection of inner thoughts and feelings we have when someone we love dies, or when we suffer another significant loss." Mourning, he writes, is "taking the grief you feel on the inside and expressing it outside of yourself" or "grief gone public."[5] These are practical definitions and they make a useful distinction.[6] Yet the important thing is to recognize that there must be an appropriate response to the pain of a loss in order for a state of wellness to be attained.

There are numerous ways to mourn, some of which will be identified later in this chapter and some of which are not lament, strictly speaking. I define *lament* in the biblical sense of a cry that addresses God. Lament is not a static exercise for, as Walter Brueggemann describes the components of lament, there is movement as we traverse the terrain of orientation in life to disorientation and eventually back, not to the same orientation but to a new orientation or reorientation. He describes the lament psalm as "a painful, anguished articulation of a move into disarray and dislocation. The lament is a candid, even if unwilling, embrace of a new situation of chaos, now devoid of the coherence that marks God's good creation."[7] Karl Barth writes, "All lament arises from the recognition of human mortality and especially the threat of separation from God."[8]

At times people suffer because of sin or poor choices they have made, and it is important to lament sins. However, prayers of lament are *not* primarily about sin, but rather about the desolation of those who pray, their belief that they have suffered unjustly, and the devastating sensation of being forsaken by God as well as by friends.[9] The biblical prayers of lament, though "irreplaceable expressions of faith," are bold, brutally honest, disturbing and paradoxical, and sometimes almost scandalous.[10] But they are effective and utterly faithful because they are honest. The form of lament not only encourages honesty, it demands honesty.

Brueggemann has compared the psalms of lament with Elisabeth Kübler-Ross's stages of grief. Lament defines the experience of suffering and provides a form for understanding and experiencing suffering. Kübler-Ross's stages on the other hand—denial and isolation, anger, bargaining, depression, and acceptance—constitute "an attempt to recover the formfulness of the grief experience."[11] Brueggemann points out the significant differences between them: "The lament expresses confidence in God's ability to intervene in the life of [God's] people. Thus the major dissimilarity in the two structures is that confession of trust leads to petition at precisely the point where in Kübler-

Ross's structure, bargaining is followed by depression."[12] The form of the biblical lament creates space for the transforming intervention of God.

Biblical Laments

Lament is the genre that most frequently occurs in the book of Psalms. There are more than twice as many psalms of lament as there are of praise, the next most frequently found genre within the Psalms.

Praise and thanksgiving are vitally important for Christian worship, but authentic worshippers cannot genuinely praise God and offer thanksgiving unless their laments are also expressed. Therefore, laments must coexist with praise and thanksgiving in worship just as they do in the book of Psalms. Might the scarcity of laments in our worship services be one reason that grieving people find it difficult to go to church?[13] My Living Well study revealed that at least 16 percent of widowed people found going to church difficult, at least for a period of time.

For people who suffer, laments to God must *precede* thanksgiving and praise in order for worship to be authentic. A task of worship is to let us hear the cry of the poor, the suffering, the bereaved, and the oppressed. A dramatic example of lament preceding praise occurred in my home congregation, College Mennonite Church in Goshen, Indiana, on September 4, 2005. It was the first Sunday after Hurricane Katrina inflicted indescribable devastation in the Gulf states. A couple in our congregation had lost a home, office building, and many valuable documents in the chaos. In addition, that week one of our members and her daughter were accused of a crime, resulting in the daughter losing custody of her two children. Our service began with laments that day, for we couldn't praise God until we acknowledged the great pain among us and in the lives of our brothers and sisters in New Orleans and the surrounding area. We sang laments in our pre-service singing and the first prayer was a long lament. We must tell and listen to the stories and laments that erupt from the despair and disorder of grief, suffering, and oppression.

Grief, suffering, and oppression are around us and within us. Fresh grief continually erupts. No matter how hard we try to ignore it, we cannot escape from loss and suffering; it is with us in our worship. How much easier, neater, and more comfortable it would be if those who suffer would express their laments in private, so that worship could be happy and pretty. But happy and pretty are not authentic. Authenticity comes only with honesty and humility. When an individual or community suffers or enters into the suffering of others and utters laments to God from that place of suffering, the individual or community can begin to experience inklings of joy in the midst of sorrow and glimpses of beauty in the rubbish of grief. Eventually, authentic thanksgiving and praise can be raised to God.

The laments in the psalms follow a pattern that allows for the ordering of raw grief, so that rather than being destructive, the grief can be transformed through its expression. The basic components to the lament are variously described, but often contain these components:

- invocation
- lament, or "the complaint"
- petition
- expression of anger
- cursing
- change or reorientation

The *invocation* names God, calling on God as though God were a friend who happens to be sovereign and who is believed to be listening. The invocation sometimes includes a question, such as "My God, my God, why have you forsaken me?" (22:1) or "O God, why do you cast us off forever?" (74:1). Interestingly, even though these laments and Jesus' cry from the cross ("My God, my God, why have you forsaken me?") indicate that the presence of God is not *felt* by the one lamenting, God is still addressed, which signifies that, by faith, the lamenter acknowledges God's presence. So already in the invocation a paradox may be heard. God is absent and at the same time present.

The second component of lament is *complaint*, which may be spoken with complaints of grief, despair, distress, sickness, guilt, persecution by enemies, or abandonment by God. The problem must be named. Giving pain a name is sometimes called the first step toward recovery. Victor Frankl writes, "Emotion, which is suffering, ceases to be suffering as soon as we form a clear and precise picture of it."[14]

A technique sometimes used when offering nursing care to people in physical pain is to invite people to rate their pain on a ten-point scale. My experience has been that when people do this, they begin to take ownership of the problem and the pain becomes manageable. It does not seem to matter whether they give the pain a five, an eight, or a ten. (And caregivers never argue, for how would we know?) Giving the pain a label defines and objectifies it, making it possible to work with it. The complaint component of lament does the same.

The complaints in the psalms are often exaggerated, couched in hyperbole. Brueggemann suggests that overstatement may be intrinsic to pain, giving the example of a hurting child who overstates a problem to get the attention of a preoccupied parent. Hyperbole may be assumed necessary to get God's attention and persuade God to act, for "often the psalmist knows God to be absent, silent, indifferent, or uncaring."[15]

The next component of lament is *petition*. Brueggemann writes, "This is the point of it all: the lament addresses God with a large, demanding, unapologetic imperative."[16] How do suffering, grieving, oppressed people bring their petitions to God? J. David Pleins points out that worshippers raise their hands in thanks to God and kneel in reverence to God. But,

> how can the brokenhearted approach God? The psalmists answer this question with profound simplicity. No special stance can be demanded of the aggrieved; we can only hope that worship makes ample room for their

cry for help. Thus it is that many of the individual laments open with a direct call to God to "rescue" or "save" the sufferer from a situation.[17]

"Come to me in my darkness, heal my broken heart," the petitioner may beg of God. Or as one intercedes for others, "Hold my loved one in your tender embrace; wrap him in the comfort of your loving presence." And as one petitions for the world, "Send your spirit of peace to Colombia and Iraq; open the eyes and ears and hearts of world leaders so that they may see and hear and know your ways of justice, peace, and love. Lord, have mercy. *Kyrie eleison.*"

Brueggemann describes two components not always present in laments: anger and cursing. Sometimes the complaint and petition are adequate expression, but under some circumstances, more is needed. The urgent petitioner is not satisfied to just petition or ask God.[18] At times words of anger are screamed at God, and although this may be uncomfortable for some, "the psalmists recognized that worship will remain a shallow affair if the worshiper's rage is left outside the sanctuary."[19] People who are hurting "may on occasion risk the unrespectable, even the unorthodox."[20] Some of these prayers are "ferocious; their blisteringly hot anger and deep hatred are completely undisguised."[21]

A modern-day example of expressing anger toward God comes to us in *A Grief Observed*, written by C. S. Lewis after the death of his wife of only a few years. He candidly expresses his doubts and anger:

> Where is God? This is one of the most disquieting symptoms. When you are happy . . . if you . . . turn to [God] with gratitude and praise, you will be—or so it feels—welcomed with open arms. But go to [God] when your need is desperate . . . and what do you find? A door slammed in your face, and a sound of bolting and double bolting on the inside. After that, silence. You may as well turn away. . . . What can this mean? Why is [God] so present a commander in our time of prosperity and so very absent a help in time of trouble?[22]

Lewis went on to say that he was less in danger of losing his belief in God than of believing dreadful things about God. "The conclusion I dread is not 'So there's no God after all,' but, 'So this is what God's really like.'"[23] In the Living Well study, forty-four people (34 percent of those who answered the question about relationship with God) named feelings and questions that are sometimes considered negative, such as feeling angry with God or losing a sense of God's presence or nearness. (This is discussed in more detail in chapter 3.)

In her introduction to *A Grief Observed*, Madeleine L'Engle applauds Lewis for "having the courage to yell, to doubt, to kick at God with angry violence," recognizing that these expressions of grief are healthy but not often encouraged. The words of Lewis are especially relevant for sincere Christians, because he had publicly defended Christianity and yet had the "courage to admit doubt about what he had so superbly proclaimed."[24]

The final component of the lament is the *change or reorientation* that occurs in the individual or group that has cried out to God. After complaints are voiced in expressions of pain and need, and after petitions are made for God's attention and intervention, demands may be shouted more vehemently. But after the venom is spewed forth, the mood and tone of the psalm changes. The negative energy has been spent and God has heard the cries. There is a characteristic positive outcome: the one who has lamented is finally satisfied and can then acknowledge, thank, and even praise God. Prayers of lament paradoxically lead to praise and hope; grief is transformed into praise and despair into hope. Explanations as to how or why this resolution comes about are not totally satisfying. Suffice it to say that here there is mystery, and yes, perhaps even miracle!

Yes, the value of the lament is more than catharsis. It does more than enable a worshipper to move to praise and thanksgiving. Transformation and miracle can occur after lamenting has run its course, as Brueggemann notes,

This utterance is a freighted theological act upon the Holy Powers of Heaven, anticipating that such speech works new reality. This speech is indeed "performative." And what it performs—requires—is a change in God's life and God's dealings with the world. One cannot join this procession of poets without imagining that grief said without apology demands that God reenter the world in a different way, at a different place, in order to do a different work. In place of "hands off," intervention. In place of indifference, transformation. In place of sustenance, miracle.[25]

Lamenting in this biblical way does indeed take us through the "stages of grief" or assists us in accomplishing the tasks of grief.

Cultural Factors in Lament

Throughout history, cultures have determined the parameters within which people normally respond to loss. Expressions of grief—or the lack thereof—vary greatly from one culture to another. I was in Puerto Rico only a few days before I learned that the expected response after a death there is for people to cry and wail and "carry on."[26] During the year that I worked in a hospital in the middle of that beautiful island, I witnessed many incidents where large groups of people gathered outside the hospital and publicly mourned together because a patient, someone with whom they had connections, had died.

Having grown up in a community with a heavy Swiss-German influence (and having Swiss-German ancestry myself), this was foreign to me. Indeed, in Northwestern Ohio people were described as "taking it well" when they showed little or no emotion after the death of a loved one.

When my father died, my mother and siblings and I were surrounded by a group of friends who said we should rejoice because our father had gone to heaven. We gathered around his casket and sang about heaven: "Until then, my heart will go on singing." I think some relatives looked on with raised eyebrows. I clearly remember my grandparents' quiet presence, sad faces, and moist eyes as they remained hour after hour in the room where their son's body lay.

When I was in my late twenties, my beloved paternal grandparents died within six days of each other. They had shared a room in a nursing home for some time before their deaths. Grandma died first, and after an afternoon visitation at the funeral home, a group of us grandchildren went to visit Grandpa. He cried and cried, and my memory is that none of us seemed to know what to say or do. We had not seen Grandpa cry before. I think we sang to him and then quickly left.

I was surprised that he was not at the funeral the next day, but did not ask about it at the time. Some years later I learned that Grandpa had expected to go to Grandma's funeral and had waited for someone to pick him up. Apparently the decision had been made that he should not be present because he might "make a scene." Three days later he died.

When my husband died, I rebelled within. I would not necessarily do what was "expected." I did not put a lid on my emotions and I did not make a scene, but I did allow honest expression of my feelings. Some people thought I was "taking it hard." I was startled when I heard this because I thought I was doing very well, that is, I was feeling and expressing in appropriate ways the pain of my loss. Bereavement includes grueling, demanding, and relentless work, and I was doing the work of grief—lamenting, expressing to God and to those around me what I was feeling—and I somehow knew that was the best thing to do.[27] Although I tried to be discreet, I refused to hide my grief.

There is no one right way to mourn; there are many right ways. However there are some wrong ways to grieve—wrong in that they do not contribute to wellness. Hope may be impossible if we respond to loss by pretending it didn't happen or by trying not to change anything.

Lament in the Church Year

Both Advent and Lent are special seasons in the church year that can offer opportunities for grieving people to give special expressions to loss and suffering. For the Christian church, Advent is a time of waiting. Suffering people may have great difficulty with the dazzle and tinsel that accompany the secular world's "holiday season." Even Christian carols don't necessarily bring joy to the suffering. But the hymns of Advent are pleas for the long-awaited Messiah to come, to free those who are held captive, to bring peace to those who suffer, to "comfort those who sit in darkness, mourning 'neath their sorrows' load," as the hymn "Comfort, comfort, O my people" articulates. I discovered that I could join in the waiting of Advent more easily than in the celebration of Christmas. The opportunity to be part of an Advent Service for Bereaved People was extremely helpful in my first year of mourning Harold's death.

Lent also took on new meaning for me during that first year. I was already introspective, and the invitation of Lent to reflect further on my walk with God was welcome. Holy Week was more intense, and by the time we got to Maundy Thursday and Good Friday, I was really living the agenda of those days, reflecting on the passion, the suffering of Jesus. In fact, I got stuck on Good Friday and was not ready for Easter Sunday. I could not lift my glad voice on high with my congregation, because I did not feel much gladness. When one kind person asked how I was, apparently wanting an honest answer, I said, "I don't *get* the question 'Where is the sting of death?' I can tell you where the sting of death is. It is here within us who mourn the loss of loved ones." She listened, nodded, and embraced me. Her response took away a bit of the sting.

As the church year went on, I found ways to lament: through my tears, cries to God, songs, and written and spoken words. We must struggle if we are to reckon with losses in our lives. Chittister writes, "Struggle is the call and the signal that we are about to renew ourselves. . . . There is only one way out of struggle and that is by going into its darkness waiting for the light and being open to new growth."[28]

During the next season of Lent my emotions were not as raw. "Take Up Your Cross and Follow Jesus" became a theme song as I studied Jesus' journey toward Jerusalem. I thought I might be ready to move beyond Good Friday that year, and I did—but only to Holy Saturday. I was in a time of waiting, and the cold dark tomb was the place to wait. It was not dissimilar to Sue Monk Kidd's cocoon, where she waited during a long dark night of her soul.[29]

Transformation slowly occurred in the tomb of my waiting. Throughout the church year that followed I used the metaphor of the tomb as I spent time with Jesus, asking my questions and pondering new life, living in the slow motion that a cool place invites, and being content with darkness. The brightness of the colorful world around me was not alluring. I needed more time to lament.

During the following season of Lent, two-and-a-half years after Harold's death, I was ready to participate in a ritual of worship in my congregation and lead a Lenten retreat. I had heard God's call to emerge from the tomb of intense mourning and lament. I preached a sermon on resurrection, and with great joy I celebrated my granddaughter's second birthday. I was able to be at peace with, and even celebrate, the rhythms of joy and sorrow and the patterns of living and dying that were part of my life.

However, I had not "gotten over" my husband's death. I believe that we never "get over it." There will always be at least a remnant of grief. We are *not* like Rachel of ancient Israel, who refuses to be comforted, but neither can we hope that our loved ones will return to us as Rachel was promised. I propose instead that we can find a source of hope in Jeremiah 31:22b, "For the LORD has created a new thing on the earth: a woman encompasses a man." This verse, which Elmer Martens refers to as the most difficult verse in Jeremiah,[30] might well be understood to mean "that the seemingly weak womanly virtues of loving and caring will achieve more than the physical strength of men."[31] Hope can be found only after lament has been expressed in weeping, refusing comfort, and perhaps even expressing rage. Hope does not come to individuals who remain composed and stoic and try to move forward with human strength, characteristics to which men have long been socialized to adhere.

The work of lament is demanding; it requires courage and initiative. The "seemingly weak womanly virtues of loving and caring" are not passive. Rachel weeps bitterly; she wails. She refuses consolation and expresses rage. Jeremiah's description of Rachel weeping for her children (see Jeremiah 31:15) may be the most powerful image of lament in the Bible. Hers is a voice of lamentation and bitter weeping, and she refuses to be comforted, because her children are no more. But through the prophet, the Lord offers hope, saying, "your children shall come back to their own country" (31:17). Rachel's lament paradoxically creates a space for the Lord to create a new thing. It is an act of faithfulness that makes possible authentic praise to God.

In the parable of the widow and the unjust judge in Luke 18, Jesus gives a justification for lamenting. The woman's persistence, faith, and trust in the unjust judge parallels the psalms of lament. In this story, Jesus clarifies that lamenting is a sign of faith, not doubt.

The Ongoing Work of Lament

The work of lament is never totally finished. After the birth of Jesus, Matthew remembers the wailing and loud lamentation of Rachel (see Matthew 2:18); so also the inequities and injustices of our lives continue to create requirements for expressions of grief. Respondent Donald shared with me that since his wife's death, as he experiences multiple other losses such as the death of siblings and friends, it seems that losses become an endless series of events. It is difficult to know which feelings belong to which loss. He compared grieving to peeling an onion.

About the time life seems to be smoother, another layer erupts, triggering more tears. Respondent Jody wrote, "I cry and then I feel relieved, not *better* but relieved."

Mennonite minister Gordon Dyck, who suffered multiple great losses throughout his life, says that he has a room in his psyche where he goes to grieve. When he is in that room, his fresh grief merges with grief from the past. All his grieving is before him at those times. It is difficult to distinguish the pain of one loss from the pain of another, and he mourns all his losses. Then the time comes when he leaves the room within himself and closes the door, knowing that he can and will open the door and go back inside when necessary. If the funeral flowers remaining from the last loss are still fresh, a new "smaller" loss may seem more intense than if the new loss came after the flowers had died and life had gone on.[32]

Experience shows that an unresolved loss will be stimulated by new losses. However, two losses do not simply hold twice as much grief as one. Rather than being the sum of parts, the grief multiplies exponentially. Those of us who have suffered one significant loss at a time cannot comprehend the intensity of grief felt by a person who has lost multiple family members within a short time, any more than someone who has not lost a loved one in death can imagine the pain that accompanies the death of a loved one.

About a year after Harold's death, three women said or implied that I was stuck in my grief and thought I needed to move on. I was startled by these responses. They are all friends—fine, educated, caring women who have also suffered losses. I tried to make sense of their perspectives, and finally I realized that they could not understand my loss because their losses were different.

Instead of being defensive and trying to explain something they would probably never understand—unless they lose a spouse in death—I expressed my feelings on paper and talked with widowed friends. Intuitively knowing that I needed to feel the pain of loss and cry buckets of tears, I often chose to sit at home in solitude, remembering and crying and trying to dream new dreams. Going out to have fun had no appeal until I began to have a taste of healing. And even when I felt I had moved a few steps forward on my grief journey, I would discover myself cycling back to where I had already traveled, for grief does not follow a linear pattern, progressing constantly toward an end goal.

One way I expressed my laments was by wearing black almost daily for a year. At first I didn't understand why I wanted to wear black, but I slowly came to realize that participating in this old tradition was a way to identify with widows throughout the world and throughout the ages (although in some cultures people wear white while in mourning). These are the amazing people who gave me hope that life would go on for me.

Except for moments (and occasionally hours) of feeling despair, my grief was mixed with hope. To express hope in the midst of sorrow, I put candles in my windows. Day after day and night after night the candles burn there, offering a glimmer of hope, suggesting there is a beacon, a guiding light in the storms of life. I continue to burn a candle in my home whenever two or three gather together, as a symbol of Jesus, the light of the world.

Eventually I came to know that it is good that some people didn't understand my feelings, for it is only in experiencing the death of a spouse that one can understand the immenseness and intensity of this grief, and I would never wish that kind of loss on anyone. My hope for my married friends is that they die together when they are old!

"Getting Over" Grief

Most pastoral-care books do not address the needs of mourners after the first year. At the same time, most books written by widowed people, along with my own research and that of others, indicates that some elements of grief will continue throughout this life.

Borrowing an image from Lewis, I was helped by thinking of Harold's death as an amputation of an extremity.[33] A part of me is gone, but I am still a whole person. I will not "get over" this amputation, but I will learn to adjust and to live without the missing part. Sometimes Harold's death seemed like an amputation of my right arm, sometimes a double amputation. (Six years later, it feels like just a pinky was amputated.)

Sixteen months after Harold's death I wrote,

> I will not get busy in order to avoid being lonely. I will experience loneliness; I will taste it and touch it. And when I have fully experienced it, I will lay it aside and go on, knowing that I have grieved well. I think the sadness will never be gone, and I wonder whether I will ever get to the "other side" of grief. Perhaps I will, but I shall always be in an arena with those who have grieved deeply, who have walked in the valley of the shadow of death. I may get through it, but I will never be totally out of sight of this grief that has shaped my life in ways that I never imagined.

The majority of widowed people seem to always carry with them some element of loss, perhaps only like a scar from an appendectomy: it is hidden for the most part but it never goes away. Only those to whom you reveal your true self (or your naked abdomen) can see the scar. And we can learn to live with scars!

One of the painful experiences that some bereaved people face is having well-intentioned people minimize the grief or tell them the grief should end within a prescribed time. Respondent Martha said, "Don't try to take my grief away. I didn't ask for this, but having been given it, I must deal with it." In addition to minimizing grief or saying it should be over, some people who want to be helpful offer premature consolation, which is futile when a person is filled with sorrow. Stopping the expressions of grief does not stop the grief itself; instead it builds a wall while the turmoil inside gathers intensity. Words of assurance must not be spoken too soon. If someone pokes a hole in a cocoon before the isolation stage has ended, the butterfly will emerge with undeveloped wings, unable to fly.

The Living Well questionnaire asked, "Since your

spouse's death, what observations have you made about the way others relate to you, such as, have you been told directly (or indirectly) that you should be 'over it'? If so, how do you respond?" One third of those who responded to this question said they had not been told to "get over it" or similar comments. Many of these expressed gratitude for the ongoing support of friends, saying they experienced sympathy and consideration. It is gratifying to know that there are many respectful and thoughtful people.

Nevertheless, some people had been told directly to "get over it." Seventeen respondents expressed some frustration with this or similar comments. When it was suggested or implied that she should be over her grief, Carla retorted, "I'm grieving as fast as I can."[34] Cynthia wanted to say, "Wait until it is your turn." Kelly wrote, "I didn't respond because I thought she doesn't know what she's talking about," and another person said, "She doesn't have a clue." Some pointed to a lack of understanding on the part of people who probably meant well but were not well informed.

A few people got the opposite response; others thought them to be grieving too fast. Still others experienced avoidance by those who apparently did not know what to say to them. Some found it hurtful that friends avoided talking about the deceased loved one.

My posing the survey question about "getting over it," seemed to trigger emotion in some respondents. For example, one person answered, "I have not, and no one had better tell me that!"

Ongoing grief is an issue even for most people who remarry. Forty-six people who had remarried[35] answered the question, "Have you continued to grieve the death of your deceased spouse within the context of your new marriage?" More than half (52 percent) stated clearly that grief had continued. The others said it did not or they weren't sure.

Not all practitioners agree that we don't get over our great losses. Zonnebelt-Smeege and DeVries are a nurse/psychologist/social worker and pastor/theologian couple who were both widowed at a young age. Together they wrote an excellent book, *Getting to the Other Side of Grief*. Although I found this book helpful and followed some of their suggestions, I was angry when I first read it. They wrote that it is possible to "get over" the death of a spouse[36] and I found myself thinking, "Sure. You two can say that because you have remarried." I don't know if I will marry again, but I determined then that if I were to write a book about grief, I would do it before another marriage! I want to be believable! I have since discovered that life for a single person can be very good. My research has shown that for most people, a new romantic relationship does not take away the pain of spousal death.

It seems that for most widowed people, making the adjustments necessary for living well after a spouse dies is a long, difficult process. Many widowed people recognize that they themselves did not know what to expect and therefore could not expect others to know what they should do or feel. There is a certain isolation in suffering and struggling. Our significant losses affect us in the depths of our souls; and although our friends offer sympathy and show compassion, they cannot really share our pain, for pain is personal. Nevertheless, the isolation of suffering is relieved when a community joins in solidarity with those who grieve. Friends (even those friends who have not been widowed) and community are vital not so much for the specific things they say or do, but for their presence, their listening ears, and their support.

Tasks of Mourning

Much is written about the stages of grief following the death of a loved one. After Elisabeth Kübler-Ross published her work with dying people in 1969, the stages of grief that she identified became the standard for students and professionals studying bereavement. By her own acknowledgment, she did not intend for those stages to describe bereavement and grief following the death of a loved one;

rather she identified the stages of a person in the process of dying.[37] The stages she described can be useful for some bereaved people, but one of the drawbacks to publishing those stages for mass consumption is that people have sometimes thought they need to grieve in a prescribed way.

I find it more useful to think of *tasks* of mourning—work that people must do after a great loss if they are to move to a place of living well. A number of authors have outlined noteworthy steps or tasks of grief.

Steven Moss describes the first of a two-step cycle of grief work:

> The realization that the loved one is gone, is dead, and nothing can change this state. It is a direct confrontation with reality. It forces the mourner to look at the hard, cold facts. . . . [There is] this sense that the mourner is going down to the grave, that he is placing himself beside the dead one. . . . It calls for a letting out of all emotions . . . [and] calls for a temporary separation from the activities of the living and of life, so that there is an actual "going down," an identification with the dead loved one.[38]

Moss goes on to describe the second step of the grief-work cycle:

> A "coming up" from the depths of the "grave." In this stage the mourner must gradually begin to form his ties again with the living and with life. . . . It must be noted that a part of the mourner will always be in the depths with the dead loved one; this is the open wound so often mentioned. Within time this part will be less and less of a weight retarding the mourner from living. . . . The reality of this part of the mourner, which is always in grief, must be acknowledged by mourner, family, friends, and minister. If it is not, confusion, embarrassment, and guilt will accompany the shedding of tears when the loved one is recalled during the forthcoming years.[39]

This process of dying and rising is succinctly stated in the words of Jesus: "Unless a grain of wheat falls into the earth and dies, it remains just a single grain; but if it dies, it bears much fruit" (John 12:24). Indeed, going down as necessary for coming up is best illustrated practically and theologically in the death and resurrection of Jesus. Living in Passion Week, especially Good Friday and Holy Saturday, is essential before one can authentically celebrate Easter. Death is not necessarily bad; in fact, death is required, crucial, indispensable for resurrection. After all, we remember the death of Jesus on *Good* Friday!

I found it helpful to mark my mourning with Joyce Rupp's four aspects of "praying a goodbye": recognition, reflection, ritualization, and reorientation.[40] Recognition begins at the time of death (or even before in some cases) and continues at deeper levels over time. Reflection overlaps with recognition as one finds ways to think about the loss and put into words what has happened. This can include journaling or telling over and over the story of what happened. Ritualization is important for expressing what words often cannot articulate. Practicing rituals helps one to connect the "outer world to [the] inner world of [the] self where the divine dwells. . . . It is there that life is gradually reoriented or given renewed direction and energy."[41] It is then and there that healing and transformation can occur. (Using rituals during bereavement is further discussed in chapter 5 of this book.) Reorientation, mixed with ritualization, happens slowly over time as one pursues, withdraws from, and then engages again in the tasks of grief.

Sidney Zisook describes the grief process in three overlapping but distinct stages:

1. Shock: denial and disbelief.
2. Acute Mourning
   a. Intense feeling states: crying spells, guilt, shame, depression, anorexia, insomnia, irritability, emptiness, fatigue;
   b. Social withdrawal: pre-occupation with health, inability to sustain usual work, family and personal relationships;
   c. Identification with the deceased: transient adoption of habits, mannerisms, and somatic symptoms of the deceased.

3. Resolution: acceptance of loss, awareness of having grieved, return to well-being, and ability to recall the deceased without subjective pain.[42]

J. William Worden, a researcher on bereavement issues, has identified the following four tasks of mourning:

1. To accept the reality of the loss.
2. To experience the pain of grief. Worden includes the often-stated truism: to get to the other side of grief we can't walk around it; we must walk through it.
3. To adjust to an environment in which the deceased is missing. In our acceptance of the reality of our loss, we must develop new skills or interests to fill the void.
4. To withdraw emotional energy and reinvest it in other activities and to memorialize the relationship.[43]

Worden suggests that although the idea may seem strange, a task of grief is to develop a new relationship with the deceased loved one. While the deceased are not physically present in person, they do have a place in the lives of survivors and that place needs to be negotiated.[44]

As long as they don't last "too long," the intense feeling states are recognized and tolerated by most grieving people and those around them. But social withdrawal by the bereaved and identification with the deceased are not as well understood or accepted. Nevertheless, there is agreement among many bereaved people and grief specialists that mourning or doing the work of grief includes "going down" or "going into" oneself, acknowledging the need for withdrawal and reflection.

In her autobiographical book *The Year of Magical Thinking*, Joan Didion writes a graphic description of what can happen during the first year after the death of a spouse.[45] She continued to relive the events of the dying of her husband, John Gregory Dunne, and the events of the following days and weeks. Her grief was complicated by the critical illness of her only child, who died just as her book went to press. Yet the illusion of Dunne's possible return with which Didion lived for that first year is not unusual. Indeed, mourning includes looking at the past. Wolfelt emphasizes the need to look into the past while finding meaning for the future.[46]

Additional thought and reflection regarding lament and the tasks of grief led me to ask what widowed people identify as the major task of grief following the death of a spouse. One-fourth of the people who answered this question said the major task was lamenting, mourning the loss, or doing the "work" of grief. They referred to feeling the pain, expressing the pain, assimilating the reality, and, very specifically, talking.

The second most frequently mentioned task of grief was finding a new identity. This was expressed in various ways, but respondent Jack expressed it well when he wrote, "Who am I without the person to whom I have been attached for so long?"

There is some overlap in the responses that named the major task as finding a new identity and those that named being alone and single again. However, identity issues have more to do with the inner work of self-discovery, while the issues of being alone and single again have to do with the social sphere. "Being alone" refers to the physical absence of another adult and "single again" is about status in society. Respondent Rhoda wrote,

> I wanted to scream. I am not SINGLE! I was married for more than half my life and in some ways I still feel married. I am not single because of never having been married. And I am not single because of divorce. I am widowed, and even though many people don't like that term, it describes my status. So why are the options on so many forms "single" or "married"? I write in my own hand in caps: "WIDOWED."

Many described the horrendous adjustment to being alone as their major task of grief. While many respondents lamented being alone, some with children at home bemoaned the fact that they had so little time to themselves. The demands of caring for grieving children while in the midst of grief are staggering. When one widowed person told me that I was lucky because I had children at home and did not have an empty house to deal with, I retorted that I would have much preferred for my husband to die after the children were "on their own." On the other hand, seeing tears fill the eyes of an eighty-something friend who was recently widowed stirred me to compassion. Six months after the death of her husband of fifty-nine years, respondent Mabel said, "It keeps getting worse!" In either case, the adjustments are great, whether they involve living alone or adjusting to life as a single parent.

Some people are not able to think about tasks of grief in an intellectual way. For them, just surviving is a major task. Respondent Norma wrote, "Just getting through each day." Jack said, "Learning to cope with life; having no one to share your thoughts with," while Jody responded, "The overwhelming feeling of trying to do everything by myself—children, work, bills, etc."

Accepting the reality of the death is the first task many grief counselors identify. Eleven respondents indicated this as the major task. Nina responded, "Facing reality; accepting that it is final." Jake wrote, "Accepting that what could have been will never have the possibility of occurring." For some widowed people, making decisions was a major task of grief. Susan was left with a business to manage and described it in this way: "I was the one making decisions; there was no one to help or do it for me."

Other widowed people identified "letting go" as a major task. "Letting go of what might have been and coming to terms with a new reality," wrote one respondent. While this is a useful image for some people, certain psychologists say that "letting go" is a poor metaphor. They challenge the concept that widowed people need to "let go so they will have energy to reinvest in new relationships. Whatever the ultimate energy that drives human life, it is not titrated as in a test tube with a limited amount for a specific relationship. . . . A new marriage does not replace the old as a new part replaces the worn part of a machine."[47]

From a sociological perspective on North America's marriage-oriented society, Helena Znaniecka Lopata names two concurrent tasks that a widow faces: "She is required through the process of mourning to detach herself sufficiently from the lost object to permit the continuation of other relationships and the development of new ones; at the same time, she has to establish for herself a new role conception as an adult woman without a partner."[48] These tasks, which also apply to widowers, are complex and for most people take a significant amount of time.

Another category of responses I identified regarding the major tasks of grief is placing the death in perspective and/or positive thinking. One example from these responses is, "Being alone and going on with life—dwelling less on the past and more on *this day* with God's help and grace."

Five respondents referred to working with memories as a task of grief: "Remembering the good memories and the not-so-good memories. Eventually the bad times fade away and the good times become something that brings warm feelings of a past time."

Another task that respondents identified could be categorized as reflecting on transformation, the work that God was doing within. Example responses include, "Trying to see death as a natural (and even good) part of everyone's journey, not to be feared in the light of Christ's ultimate victory in which we participate by God's grace," "Asking what does God want to teach me through my loss," and "Transformation of the self so that the experience enriches rather than destroys and one becomes more than one could have otherwise become."

The task of finding new interests or reviving old ones helped other widowed people. One respondent put the major task in terms of helping others experiencing loss; another began making quilts for her children and grandchildren. One person identified that keeping busy was a major task. This might be a red flag. To be busy doing the work of grief is one thing, but to find ways to be busy so that grief and mourning can be avoided is not a healthy behavior.

As might be expected, some bereaved people named unresolved issues such as family resentments and suppressed guilt that needed attention after the death. One respondent said a major task was "trying to cover up my true feelings to my family." Another said, "My spouse hated me." Lament for these kinds of situations is rarely addressed but it is one to which caring people will attempt to attend.

Lament is an effective way to respond to loss and suffering. However, it is not an end in itself. The goal is healing. Lament facilitates healing by assisting suffering or bereaved people to move from a place of muteness to a place where pain can be expressed. It allows bereaved people to express the pain of loss and to ask the necessary questions.

It is helpful to understand the elements of lament, but understanding is not a way around lament. The work of lament needs to be done with each loss. One woman reported that when she suffered a proportionally much smaller loss several years after being widowed, it seemed huge, and again doing the work that grief demands was strenuous and challenging. Will I suffer more and more losses as life goes on? Absolutely. Can I prepare for them? I do not know. I do know I will need to mourn, to lament each loss so that I can move along on life's journey. And maybe as time goes on, I will be able to discover more quickly the gift that is hidden in the loss, the joy in the sorrow, the "grace disguised."

Time Heals All?

It has been said that time heals a broken heart. I do not believe that. It is not *time* that heals. Others say that mourning heals a broken heart. Is this true? Is it what we *do* with the grief that leads to healing? That is part of it. The expression of feelings is crucial, but simply exposing feelings is not enough to dispel the gloom, remove the pain, or stop the suffering. We can heal only if we lament. And the pattern of biblical lament includes necessary ingredients for healing: expressions to God about the pain and anger caused by the loss and the recognition of a purpose in life.

Recognition of a purpose seems to be essential for healing from a significant loss or surviving great suffering. In his story of Jews in concentration camps during the Holocaust, Frankl said that those who survived did so because they had something to live for, something beyond themselves. Or simply put, hope! Those without hope died.[49] There is hope in the invocation of the biblical lament—as one addresses God—and in the conclusion of the lament. At both of these times, God is acknowledged. When God is recognized, we come to understand a bit more about who we are, particularly who we are in relation to God. And in that relationship, a purpose in life, or hope, begins to emerge.

But it is not time or mourning or hope that heals a broken heart. Time, mourning, and hope are all necessary. But God does the healing. God created us in such a way that, by God's grace—usually extended through loving people—we have the capacity to pick up the pieces of a heart that is broken in sadness and a self that is shattered with pain. This is not healing without scars, but it is healing in the sense that we can live a meaningful life with at least a portion of peace and joy.

—3—

Learning and Transformation

What lies behind us and what lies before us
are tiny matters compared to
what lies within us.
— Ralph Waldo Emerson[1]

Becoming empty is a step in the process of transformation,
not empty in the sense of being barren,
but empty in the sense of being a liminal space
that is full of possibilities.
— Urban T. Holmes III[2]

Emptier, fill me
More full emptiness always
Filler, empty me.
— Joan Yoder Miller[3]

Life is a series of lessons,
some of them obvious, some of them not.
Life is a balancing act
lived between the poles of unreasonable hope on one hand
and disheartening disquiet on the other.
— Joan Chittister[4]

Learning to live and love and die is the great human task. Kathleen Norris suggests that to take on one (life, love, or death) may be to accept all three. Maturing means that we need to reject much of the popular mythology "that life is simply handed to us, that love is easy, . . . and death a subject to be avoided altogether."[5] In spite of the strenuous work that grief demands, I have learned that a journey in grief is an outstanding opportunity to learn about oneself, to grow in relationship to God, and to gain clarity about some of life's most important issues.

Joan Chittister writes, "It is only vulnerability that prepares us to live well, to understand others, and to take our proper place in the human enterprise."[6] This offers great hope to a bereaved person, for the death of a spouse exposes many layers of vulnerability. If Chittister is right, if being vulnerable prepares us to live well, perhaps that is why it is possible to live a more meaningful life after being widowed. I indeed have found life to be deeper and richer since my husband's death. I wouldn't choose nor would I wish on anyone widowhood as a means to a more meaningful life, but when it happens, one has a unique opportunity for growth.

Along with being a place of vulnerability, bereavement is also a place of liminality. *Liminality* is defined as the time between life and death, an in-between time or space where one moves "out of the structure where order and predictability provide a sense of security" to a time or place of anti-structure "where we face [an] awareness of the chaos that surrounds us." It is a middle place, where old categories no longer work and new ways are not yet discovered. All descriptions of liminality include an experience of loss of some kind, a transition time of contradictions, preparation for transformation, and eventually a new equilibrium and reintegration into life as a changed person. Another description of liminality is a place "between two worlds, one dead and the other powerless to be born."[7]

Experiencing the death of a loved one is a "profoundly spiritual issue that disturbs and awakens our souls." The death of a loved one is a crisis, and psychologists know that people in crisis are in a "state of heightened psychological and spiritual sensitivity that makes them less defensive and more open to change."[8] In fact, we cannot *not* change.

When life is going smoothly for us, it is easy for us to be satisfied with a superficial relationship with God. But when suffering disrupts our life, upsetting our equilibrium and throwing us for a loop, we may become more motivated to do serious soul searching.[9] There is indeed much that can happen in a liminal space. But in this sacred space, a mourning person does not have to necessarily *do* something. One can just be and rest in the mystery of God, "supported by the life-breath of God." A spiritual guide can assist one in discerning when it is time to *do*, but "before we can affirm that death is a turning point inviting us to discern how we will live, the fullness of the death must be experienced."[10] That can include lamenting and finding activities, words, and rituals to express the sting and pain of death.

Our culture is uncomfortable with death. So, unfortunately, rather than "encouraging people to enter the time of chaos, contradiction, and liminality even more deeply and naming and lamenting what [has died or] is dying, [we want people to get] out of crisis and on with their lives as quickly as possible."[11] But there are no shortcuts.

One of the claims of many people, which can be heard in conversations and read in books, is that there is no right or wrong way to grieve or mourn. I do not agree with that statement. There are many "right" ways to mourn, ways that are appropriate and effective and are means of growth. However, there are some "wrong" ways to mourn. One can answer the call to enter into the pain, walk alone into the darkness, embrace the grief, and lament with body, heart, and soul. Or one can try to hide from the pain and slowly become eroded by the gnawing, unexpressed grief.

Denial is a coping mechanism that allows a bereaved person to absorb the reality of a loss little by little. Some level of denial is normal and expected for a time and is not unhealthy. But if the denial goes on indefinitely, problems will arise. People who deny their grief and try to replace the love object without processing the loss will eventually have difficulties.

If a person refuses to express grief or is not allowed an obvious expression of grief, it will build up and find an outlet that may be undesirable. One person I know could not cry after the death of a loved one, but she had diarrhea off and on for months. The diarrhea finally stopped when she began to cry. A man in his seventies has a stuttering problem that he thinks started after the death of his mother. He was five years old and nobody would talk to him about what had happened. Many years later, he is now trying to find ways to mourn that loss. A widow finds she has not cried much since her husband's death. When asked about earlier losses, she talked about her mother's death when she was seven years old. She remembers crying and crying, but "it didn't do any good." Consequently, she now finds ways other than crying to express her grief. These include writing and working in her yard.

The goal of mourning or doing the work of grief is to return to fullness of life, integrating the loss into a life that has changed and expanded. The work of grief helps one adapt to what cannot be changed and at the same time explore what can be.

As we lament or mourn our losses in liminal spaces, we will likely be introspective. Lamenting is not necessarily finished when introspection begins, but introspection and lament will overlap, just as do recognition and reflection in Joyce Rupp's aspects of praying a goodbye. Introspection and reflection at a time of loss lead to new insights about the self. Throughout the ages, from Socrates to Nouwen, the importance of "knowing yourself" has been emphasized. Some say we cannot know God until we know ourselves. Others say when we truly know ourselves, we will know God, for we have been created in the image of God. Thomas Merton said, "When we find our true selves we find God, and when we find God we find our true selves."[12]

Rupp asserts that finding our true selves is a "life-long process of transformation that leads to greater compassion and connection with the world" beyond ourselves. "Becoming our true selves" is not an easy process.[13] Busyness and lack of introspection interfere with the challenging work of discovering God and our true selves.[14] However, life's routines come to a screeching halt when a beloved dies, and one is presented with the opportunity for introspection, reflection, and eventual transformation.

Meaning of Life and Death

One cannot have a close brush with death, either one's own near-death experience or the death of a loved one, without contemplating the meaning of life. At the same time, some widowed people are so consumed with the tasks of day-to-day survival after being widowed that for many months there is no time to reflect. This tends to be true particularly for parents of young children and in the case of a sudden death. But eventually the questions about the meaning of life will surface. Facing questions may be like hitting a brick wall; one's attention is demanded. Many bereaved people discover that only after looking at the meaning of death can they go on with life, living fully.

The death of a loved one is a unique category of loss in which we come to recognize that our lives are intimately dependent on others for meaning and significance. We are called to embrace themes of unforeseen events, to face questions that challenge us to the core, questions that bring to consciousness "the contextual and finite themes of our lives."[15] At some level we need to "relearn the world," a task that "remains at all times a process in which we are involved, not one that we complete or finish."[16] We may have lived with the illusion of control, but here we face personal limitations, our inherent vulnerability, our own mortality.

Spiritual guides call bereaved people to enter humanity's struggle to be present to the mysteries of God and to participate in the engagement of the Divine Spirit and the human spirit. Karl Rahner said that to speak of the human is to speak of the divine and vice versa.[17]

> God is the depth dimension in experiences such as solitude, friendship, community, death, hope and, as such, is the orientation toward the future. Rahner goes so far as to say that loneliness, disappointments and the ingratitude of others can be graced moments because they open us to the transcendent. The silence of God, the toughness of life and the darkness of death can be graced events. The mystery of grace discloses itself as a forgiving nearness, a hidden closeness, our real home, a love which shares itself, something familiar which we can turn to from the alienation of our own empty and perilous lives. When we are in touch with ourselves authentically, we experience God.[18]

Embracing grief and engaging in the struggle that loss dispenses to us requires that we ask the difficult questions of life, the questions that philosophers and theologians and ordinary people have asked throughout the ages. A word of caution is in order here. "Going deep" may evoke issues that require careful guidance. An experienced spiritual director, therapist, or pastoral counselor may be very helpful in dealing with life-shaking issues.

Grief Journey as a Spiritual Journey

A journey in grief following the death of a loved one is simultaneously a spiritual journey. Not all people may recognize it as such, but those who ask the typical questions about life and death will discover they are on a spiritual quest. One's attention is demanded by the void that the death of a dearly loved one creates within a person's being. One widow said, "I felt like my heart had been split wide open—and I believe that 'helped' create a deeper relationship with God." Another response to a death is "to go mystical," which George MacLeod says is not to turn away from the affairs of the world, but to "go more deeply into life, to find God at the heart of life . . . and to liberate God's goodness" within oneself and in one's relationships.[19]

The grief I experienced following Harold's death plunged me into the depths of my being, depths I had not known existed. There, in my pain and anguish and lament, I met God. God, in whose image I had been created, was always there, although sometimes ignored by me. In my aloneness, I knew a new kind of communion with God, and in that divine, holy, loving, sustaining presence, words were not needed. I met God at a place where the boundaries are gone and an unexplainable oneness exists. In this mysterious oneness I am fully known, loved, and accepted, and have a sense of approaching spiritual union with God.

The Longing Within

Christians have long recognized the yearning for God that exists within the human soul. Philosophers, psychologists, and theologians describe in various ways the phenomenon of the human need for a relationship with God. Some call it a God-shaped vacuum or void in our lives. Psychoanalyst Judith Viorst refers to our lifelong yearning for union, suggesting that this yearning originates in our desire as infants to return to the womb or to a state of symbiosis or illusionary union.[20] If we consider this perspective from the human sciences, we also need a more fundamental view, such as the one simply expressed in St. Augustine's quote "Our hearts are restless until we find our rest in God."

James Loder writes on this concept:

> The great human difficulty is that the human spirit has been separated from its ultimate ground in the Spirit of God. It has a measure of constructive power, but without its proper ground, it becomes a loose canon of creativity. In its bewildered, blundering brilliance, it cries out for wisdom to an "unknown God." But it is the personal Author of the universe whose Spirit alone can set the human spirit free *from* its proclivity to self-inflation, self-doubt, self-absorption, and self-destruction, and free *for* its "magnificent obsession" to participate in the Spirit of God and to know the mind of God. . . . The human spirit searches the human mind, and so the

human mind comes to know itself through its spirit. . . .
Apart from the Spirit-to-spirit communication of the
mind of God, the attempt of the human mind to know
itself, to say nothing of knowing the mind of God, is
utter foolishness [1 Corinthians 2:10].[21]

The authors of *Remembering Our Home* promote the
idea that we all come from the heart of God, which is our
true home and that we were known by God even before
conception. They give anecdotal evidence that many children up to age five have some memories of their life with
God before they were born.[22] This reference supports the
idea that there is a memory within people of prebirth symbiosis.

Perhaps the lifelong yearning for union that Viorst
describes is really a longing for re-union with God. This
may parallel the longing to return to the womb, because it
is through our mother's womb that we come from the heart
of God to our existence as separate individuals in this
world. Envisioned or understood in this way, death is a
return to our first home, where God, from whose heart we
came, awaits us as a most loving parent awaits his or her
children.

Whether we identify the longing or restlessness within
ourselves to be fulfilled only by resting in God, by return-
ing to our true home or by some other phenomenon, many
thoughtful people recognize some kind of unsatisfied desire
within themselves. Richard Rohr describes this desire as
fulfilled only when we enter through the "gate of the temple" into the "holy of holies," where God resides. He further says that in an intimate friendship with another person
or in a good sexual relationship we can go *to* the gate of
the temple, but it is only in relationship with God that we
can go into the holy of holies. (Rohr goes on to say that a
good sexual relationship or intimate friendship can take
away our anxiety long enough so that we can find out what
it is we really desire.)[23]

Nature abhors a vacuum and will always try to fill it.
Our culture tells us that sex and material possessions will

satisfy. And indeed some married people find that in their imperfect relationships with their spouses, many yearnings for union are at least partially met. However, for some, a relationship with a spouse can interfere with a deepening relationship with God.

Mari, a respondent to the Living Well survey, said that she did not realize how she had tried to fill her deepest longings with her marriage relationship until after her husband, Gene, died. She recognized within herself a void that could not be filled by any person and realized that some of the restlessness in her marriage had occurred because she was trying to fill that void with Gene, the man whom she loved and respected.

In response to Mari's complaints about his imperfections, Gene had once told her it seemed like she wanted him to be Jesus. She had backed off and playfully agreed that she did want him to be *like* Jesus. After Gene's death, Mari came to realize that he had made an astute observation: The void that she had attempted to fill by working for a "perfect" marriage with a "perfect" man could be filled only by God. She eventually identified that a gift of Gene's death was the opportunity to see herself more clearly and to grow in her relationship with God so that she could finally enter the "holy of holies."

This experience of spiritual growth and transformation for Mari took place over a period of years. Time is necessary for gaining new understandings of the self and, in this case, for moving from a head knowledge of the importance of having God at the center of life to understanding and comprehending it from experience.

Transformation cannot be rushed. This is one reason why remarrying quickly after the death of a spouse is usually not advised. Mari learned that when she found herself in a romantic relationship with another man, she did not work at her issues of new growth. That relationship ended, and although she was very disappointed and had another loss to grieve, she eventually recognized that if she had married that person, she would have been trying to replace

Gene, wanting her new husband to be the perfect husband that Gene could never be. Mari would have bypassed the opportunity to learn to know deep within herself that only God can fill her greatest longings. In addition, she would likely have been very frustrated in her new marriage.

The above story is an example of the deep intertwining of sex, death, and spirituality as described by Loder.[24] The connectedness of sexuality and spirituality are profound to the extent that the giving of oneself sexually is not unlike giving up one's life both spiritually—as in vowing one's life in service to God—and physically at the time of the death of the body.

In analyzing human development in theological perspective, Loder refers to Freud's Oedipal developmental stage (three to five years of age) as focusing on "sex, death, and the origin of worship."[25] Loder notes that Freud probably overemphasized the sexual components and states that "the central issue at stake in this period is not sex role identity, but the quest of the human spirit for being-outside-oneself [and] sexuality is but one aspect of it."[26]

Loder goes on to say that the drive for the human spirit to be outside itself is a spiritual drive that

> gives rise to culture and ultimately to worship of a god who, though being truly Other, at the same time provides ultimate meaning for the concrete particulars of everyday life. Then worship is not a neurotic flight from a threatening past but a creative response to a future that is known in the present through the irrepressible transcendent and transformative capacity of the human spirit as it receives its power, identity, and the whole of the created world as a daily gift from God. Developmentally this drive is a longing that anticipates but does not yet know the Face of God until it is revealed in the image of God in Jesus Christ. This is a revelation that must be grasped and appropriated Spirit-to-spirit, as the awakening of the human spirit at this period of development makes evident.[27]

Reflecting on the similarities and differences between the longing to know God (or see the face of God) and to know and be known sexually can lead to tremendous growth in understanding self and God. Both reflect a deep longing that may become a more conscious reality after the death of a spouse. (This will be discussed further in chapter 4.)

Relationship with God

An important insight into a person's grief journey comes from learning about her or his image of God and relationship with God. The Living Well questionnaire asked, "How did your spouse's death affect your relationship with God?"

A small number said that the death did not affect their relationships with God. One wrote, "I understood on a rational level that life works by natural laws and is often unpredictable and tough. God is God nonetheless."

Of those who replied to this question, many said God seemed far away, others confessed they were angry with God, and a handful stated that they could not pray or had difficulty praying. Others articulated their questions:

- I know that God has the power to have stopped the accident, so why did God allow it?
- I wondered if I was being punished or if my wife was punished.
- Her death tested my views in regard to prayer. Hundreds of people had prayed for her healing, yet healing did not happen.

I find it remarkable that the 34 percent who chose to answer this question had the courage to name feelings and questions that are sometimes considered "negative." Most people feel some anger with or distance from God when a loved one dies, especially if the death was "untimely." This may be "the dark night of the soul" about which many of the ancient and medieval mystics wrote. Chittister says, "This dark night [is] a necessary moment in the development of the soul. Sure of the absence of God, we actually become aware of the presence of God. It is the paradox of faith."[28]

spondents to the questionnaire expressed their places
kness in ways that seemed to be variations on a few
themes: I was angry with God, God seemed far away, and
I could not pray. One cannot communicate very well with
a God who seems distant or silent, so if God is nowhere to
be found, it is difficult or impossible to pray. But those who
enter the darkness, engage in the struggle, and articulate
the difficult emotions, find they can eventually move along.

One respondent aptly described the struggle in the darkness: "I felt the 'silence' of God many times and for a long
time. I longed for and cried out to God for comfort and did
not feel a response. It was terribly hard to praise or hear
others praise God. Yet I was always yearning for direction
from God, wanting to find purpose in life again." These
words are reminiscent of Jesus' cry from the cross, "My
God, my God, why have you forsaken me?" Although feeling forsaken by God, Jesus and the above person both cried
out to God. There was an underlying faith that God was
present and would hear, even though God's presence was
not *felt*.

The presence of God became more important and more
meaningful for the majority of respondents while they
mourned the death of their spouses. Some named an
awareness of God's presence. Many said they felt closer to
God after the spouse's death than they had before, and others said their relationship with God had grown.

Ongoing Changes in the Relationship with God

A second question in this area of the survey asked widowed people if their relationship with God continued to
change. Fifty-one percent of those who responded to this
part said it continued to change in positive ways. Some said
yes with emphasis. One elaborated, "I'm moving into a
sense of God's presence within, a sense of oneness with
God and others." Others described the relationship with
God as stronger, deeper, closer, or more intimate, while
some described changes like a richer devotional life, taking

more time to pray and nurture the spiritual life, and being open to the possibility of new callings and direction in life. Another noted learning that the hard questions can be left unanswered, and one said, "I've developed a deep sense of God's presence and care, especially in retrospect." Another wrote, "I am now aware that life has both joys and sorrows and God is with us through all of it."

Thirteen respondents gave a somewhat tentative yes, saying, "I hope that I have grown in faith and love for God," and "I probably have a closer relationship with God." Another said, "I believe I have grown spiritually," and another, "I've come beyond my anger with the circumstances and can now enjoy communion of God again—although my joy has not returned."

One respondent said she was drawn to the experience of her mother, who was widowed with seven small children. She said, "My children were already grown and were a pillar of strength for me. I felt strengthened just remembering my mother and her deep faith in God."

Integrating Loss into Life

Loneliness is an enormous issue for many widowed people. When asked to identify the most difficult tasks after spousal death, dealing with loneliness was a common answer. Many said "adjusting to being alone" or "missing my spouse" was most difficult. Others referred to feeling an emptiness or a void. Spouses obviously fill an important psychological space for many people. When the spouse dies, what happens to that space? For many it remains empty for a time and then is slowly filled. Others try to fill it quickly. Yet one woman who was widowed more than ten years said she keeps within herself a reserved lonely space that has never completely filled. In another study, 25 percent of young widows surveyed said that loneliness was their most serious problem.[29]

However, even loneliness can be seen as an invitation to transformation, according to authors Jacqueline Syrup

Bergan and S. Marie Schwan, who write, "The abyss of human aloneness and fear has always eluded adequate expression, yet ironically this very experience of intimate and intense suffering serves as the caldron of heroism and creativity."[30] Struggling with loneliness is part of the work of grief—not accepting it passively, but while living within it, being alert to new life that may grow out of the loneliness. The ability to tolerate being alone may develop during widowhood as one faces a deep level of aloneness. "Paradoxically, the ability to be alone is the condition for the ability to love," writes Erich Fromm. New dimensions of loving are available to those who cultivate the ability to be alone. Fromm also said that people who love "are with each other by being one with themselves, rather than by fleeing from themselves."[31]

To find space to be alone is a challenge for some. Many widowed people discover they need to practice selective socializing. There is simply not enough energy to do all the things that they might want to do or think is expected. When I dropped off my daughter for a basketball game two years after Harold's death, an old friend asked why I was not staying. I said I had things to do at home. He said, "Oh come on. Now that you don't have a man dragging you around you should have plenty of time."[32] I thought, "Apparently you have not considered the fact that I am now a single mother and a single head of household. I take care of the children and the house and the cars and the yard and the bills—things most couples share." But I didn't say that. Neither did I try to explain that it took time and energy to find the courage to dream new dreams and to figure out who I was as a single person. Instead I answered, "What makes you think I don't have a man in my life?"

Perhaps this is an example of someone not knowing what to say to a widowed person. Even though his comment seemed inappropriate, I was glad he spoke to me, and maybe that is why I gave him a playful answer. On another occasion I told him about some of my struggles and he listened with compassion.

For years after being widowed I practiced selective socializing. Going to weddings was difficult, so I planned carefully. I did not want the wedding families to feel sorry for me on that day or to be sorry they had invited me. I turned down some invitations and realized I was not required to have a reason that others would understand. At the first wedding I attended after Harold's death, I arranged to sit with other widowed people during the reception. During another reception, when I realized I could no longer hide the intense sadness I was feeling, I quietly left—and just in time! I had no more than gotten to my car when my body began to convulse in sobs.

Selective socializing for me has meant responding to the need for a balance of solitude and activity, and then choosing the activities that are nurturing and life-giving. I know the fragility of life as I did not know before, and life is too short to choose to do things that are unrewarding. Only when I have attended to my inner needs am I ready to participate in events for the benefit of others.

Part of the challenge of integrating loss into life is that there is much mystery to encounter. Death is mysterious, our sexuality is mysterious, and there is mystery in our relationship with God. Robert Morneau makes connections between mystery and loneliness, pointing to some clarity that paradoxically leaves us stuttering and stumbling, figuratively and literally.

> Mystery is necessarily lonely because of its profundity, not its incomprehensibility. Nothing is more meaningful than mystery in its essence, but because of our finite minds and constricted hearts, mystery throws us into the land of loneliness. Standing on the ocean shore, even surrounded by friends, . . . draws us deep into the darkness of not knowing infinity; gazing at the horizon from a mountain peak plunges our imaginations into the experience of immensity; contemplating the fingers of a newborn child or pondering the death of a life-time friend—the mysteries of life and death—drives us into an inarticulateness. Mystery means not to know and that space is lonely. No one can enter into the uniqueness of our expe-

rience even though blessed with compassion. All of us stutter and stumble in the presence of a sunset, a friendship, a star. Such is life.[33]

Ronald Rolheiser points out that within our aching loneliness and restlessness is a screaming cry to move outward, to seek activities that will soothe our existential loneliness, of which we may become more aware when we lose a life partner. However, he says, "ultimately what turns our restless aching into inner quiet and peace is not more activity, but sitting still long enough for restlessness to turn to restfulness, compulsion to freedom, impatience to patience, self-absorption to altruism, and heartache to empathy."[34] Loneliness is an invitation to solitude, and within solitude we may find ways to integrate loss into our lives.

Reframing the Questions

After living with the questions "Why did this happen?" or "Where is God?" or "Why me?" many bereaved people are eventually ready to move on to new questions or to reframe the old ones. Instead of "Why me?" the question may become "Why not me?" Instead of "Why did this happen?" the question may be "What can I learn from this?" Perhaps instead of asking, "Where is God?" one might ask, "How can I come to know more about God through my loss?" The old questions may lead to dead ends; the new questions may be life-giving.

The psychological work of a widowed person is described well by Loder in what he describes as a "turn inward at the ego level [which] means reassessing one's developmental history, discovering one's own voice, and using new resources to re-envision the future."

> What is involved is termination, individuation, and initiation: termination of the old . . . patterns . . . that bind one to the past; individuation, a Jungian term that can be succinctly stated in the phrase "becoming one's own person"; and initiation, which means drawing on new resources for constructing a future—not only one's own, but for subsequent generations.[35]

Psychiatrist Sidney Zisook describes how bereaved people often experience a significant or even radical alteration of their worldview:

> Following their loss, the bereaved are frequently floundering for direction, often well into the second year. This loss of direction and meaning is precipitated by the disruption of the plans and hopes they shared with their spouse, or by shattering of belief systems which governed many of their actions: beliefs in being able to control one's destiny, maintain invincibility, belief in a just and merciful God, deferred gratification, and unbounded optimism. All such beliefs are challenged, fall short, and leave a vacuum that only gradually becomes filled again—at times with modified reassertions of the old beliefs, and at times with totally new ones, reflecting the finiteness and fragility of life and the limits of control. As a result, the bereaved often become more appreciative of daily living, more patient and accepting, and more giving. They may develop new careers or change them, enjoy themselves with more gusto, or find new outlets for creativity. On the other hand, some people do stagnate or wither, unable to meet the challenges, unable to experience personal growth.[36]

The invitation to all is to confront and struggle with issues that arise and not to get stuck in the questions. Each bereaved person must wrestle with his or her own questions and the timing for asking them. Friends and relatives as well as books and other resources help bring discernment regarding when it is time for a bereaved person to move on. However, only that person really knows when it is time to turn a corner.

Timing Considerations for Mourning

There is no question that mourning the death of a loved one takes a long time—maybe even a lifetime. One wise and articulate widowed man said that "time itself is distorted by catastrophic loss, so I am hesitant to talk about time at all. In one sense, the healing process begins immediately. At least it did for me. But it continues to this day [more than ten years later]. It will take a lifetime. But I would say the most immobilizing grief occurred over the first two years." He went on to say, "The sign to me of some measure of productive healing is when the person who has suffered loss is learning to integrate the experience into the landscape of his or her life and thinking in terms of enlargement rather than reduction." He said that the loss began to play a less important role after he decided to work at integrating the loss rather than trying to somehow overcome it or recover from it. The challenge for a widowed person is to adjust to a life that was not chosen but must be embraced.

How long does it take until loss is no longer the "major theme" of a widowed person's life? Does each year get easier than the year before? The Living Well study yielded an interesting range of answers.

First and Second Years After the Death of a Spouse

In the Living Well questionnaire, widowed people were asked if they had been able to separate themselves from the deceased spouse to the extent that grief was no longer the major theme of life, and if so, when that happened. Twenty-five people said that it was during the first year after the death that life moved on so that grief was no longer the major theme of life. Thirty-two people said it was at one year that grief was no longer the major theme. One said, "Grief was not the major theme but it was still very strong; at times it reoccurred quite strongly, but gradually faded." Another stated, "It's a daily part of life but not the major theme." Twenty-seven people said that by two years grief was no longer the major theme. One person said, "When I began planting flowers again I knew a major shift had come!" Responses are detailed in chart 1.

Chart 1

GRIEF NO LONGER THE MAJOR THEME	Total people	% of those who said yes	Women	Men
Within first year	25	18.5%	14	10
At about one year	32	24%	19	12
At about two years	27	20%	20	7
At about three years	30	22%	20	10
At about four years	3	2%	3	0
At about five years	6	4%	5	1
Seven to eight years	2	1.5%	2	0

Again, there is a wide range of what is normal in the "work of grief" and its timing. One of the assumptions often made following the death of a loved one is that grief will gradually diminish and eventually be gone. Many informed people will allow for the anniversary dates and holidays to be times of brief relapses into grief, but after being through the "firsts," they think it should be smooth sailing.

I was one of those individuals who expected the second year after my husband's death to be much easier than the first. I remember thinking about four months into my grief journey that if I could just fast-forward one year into the future, life would be so much easier. Then I saw a friend whom I had not seen since Harold's death. This friend had just passed the first anniversary of his wife's death, so my first question to him was, "Is the second year easier?" I fully expected he would say yes, but instead his reply was, "No, not easier, but different." The harsh reality of a long, difficult journey was just setting in for me.

My second year of widowhood was a year of ups and downs. I was no longer experiencing the numbness that often hung over me like an invisible cloud during the first several months after Harold's death. I had found some new joy, particularly in the birth of my first grandchild. My life had a new focus in that I had become a student. But there were still times of deep sadness and seemingly insatiable longing for what was missing. During the second year, anger reared its unwanted head and I had to find new ways to deal with it. The challenges of the second year were great for me.

Based on my experience, it came as no surprise that many people who responded to my questionnaire found the second year to be more difficult than the first. Of the 120 who answered the question comparing the first and second years of bereavement, 30 percent said the second year was easier, while 26 percent said it was not much different from the first year. Another 26 percent said that the second year was not easier or harder than the first, but different. Four of these had remarried, which suggests that marriage does not necessarily make the grief journey easier.

Sixteen percent of those who answered this question said that the second year was more difficult than the first. This included 20 percent of the women but 5 percent of the men. One woman underlined the word *difficult* twice. The most frequently cited reason was that reality had set in. Receiving less support made the second year more difficult for others. Some referred to practical issues and others mentioned the difficulty of the second set of holidays.

These responses confirm that even though life can be, and usually is, good again, the work of lamenting and mourning is not completed after one or even two years. One person described the pain increasing over time. He said, "I have felt the pain of this loss every day for all these months, and it's like each day's pain piles up on all the pain I already have felt, making it feel like more and more pain."

The Zisook study of three hundred widowed people showed that for many, the course of grief was much longer than expected. "Although dysphoric feelings such as depression and anxiety tended to diminish over time, they did not do so to a statistically significant degree and often remained present even four or more years after the death."[37] That project included a self-rated overall adjustment to widowhood. At the end of thirteen months, 32 percent of widows and widowers said they had made an excellent overall adjustment; after twenty-five months, 40 percent had made an excellent adjustment; and after thirty-seven months, 50 percent had adjusted well. This shows that 50 percent of people in this study thought that they were not well adjusted at three years after spousal death. After four years, 20 percent rated their adjustment to widowhood as either fair or poor.[38] These findings have implications for pastoral care, which will be discussed in chapter 5.

Gifts of Grief

Many people eventually discover a gift or gifts somewhere along the journey of grieving a loss. Some speculate that bereavement may stimulate heightened levels of creativity, noting that many artists, writers, and musicians have experienced great losses. Indeed, there is an old Chinese that says, "Sorrow brews poets."

The Living Well questionnaire states that many bereaved people eventually find a gift or gifts in grief and then asks, "Have you experienced some gift(s) that you can name?" Eighty-six percent of those who answered this question named gifts they had received. Of the eleven people whose spouses had died in the previous year, two could already name a gift:

- •Compassion for others that are hurting and empathy for them are emotions that I can now share more freely
- •Personal growth, doing things I never knew I could, feeling stronger

Forty-two percent of those who responded affirmatively to this question identified that they experience more compassion or sympathy for other grieving people and recognized this as a gift.

Many respondents named personal growth, more independence, or greater freedoms as gifts. Others named spiritual growth. People do not choose losing a spouse as a means to personal or spiritual growth, but these responses show that transformation can occur. One of the most poignant responses was, "Now that my spouse is gone I have to 'blossom' another side of me that was not there before." What a beautiful metaphor for transformation! The respondent obviously took some responsibility for growth in saying, "I have to blossom," while at the same time seemed to recognize the part that Creator God played in what was happening.

Spiritual growth includes facing questions of life and death that arise at the time of the death of a loved one, as well as learning about the connections between joy and sorrow. Experiencing the death of a spouse led a number of respondents to experience in new ways that life is a gift.

Along with recognizing and accepting gifts of grief may come the notion of "holy indifference," an awareness of the many gifts of God and an openness to receive them. Chittister writes that the key to living well is "detachment from the idea that there is only one way . . . to go through life joyfully."[39] Other keys include appreciating what is and being open to whatever comes.

Although many bereaved people eventually discover some kind of gift through the total experience of loss, it is inappropriate to tell someone that at the time of the death of a loved one. When one newly bereaved man was told that there would be a gift in his experience, he angrily replied that he didn't want such a gift.

Finding a New Identity

Discovering who I am is a lifelong process. Normal development includes stages in which identity questions come to the fore in new ways. This is recognized particularly during the turbulence of adolescence, often during young adulthood, and sometimes in the middle adult years.

The questions of identity may be greater when a marriage ends than at any other time in life. My identity was *not* all wrapped up in my husband. I did not identify myself as Mrs. Harold Hartzler. I was Rachel Hartzler. I had jobs and numerous interests that were not connected with Harold. Nevertheless, part of my identity was being a married woman.

"I'm a widow" were the first words that came out of my mouth when I was told Harold had died. It was October 6, 1999, about 6 p.m., two hours after Harold had kissed me goodbye and gone out jogging. Upon arriving at the hospital I was told that Harold had died and the nursing supervisor asked me whom she should call. I was unable to answer her for a few moments. I first had to establish who I was in this swirling sea of images and memories, shock and confusion, fears and broken dreams. I was a widow, and I had to say it out loud.

Although mourning took precedence in my life for many months, I began taking on a new identity as a widow. It seemed to be part of the loss. Four months later, when a formerly widowed friend asked me if I was beginning to grieve the loss of my marital status, I did not know what she was talking about. My losses were all mixed together and my grief was for everything that I had lost. Several months later I recognized what she was referring to: losing status as a married woman is a multilayered loss.

Without giving much thought to the decision, I began using Nafziger, my maiden name, as my middle name. It seemed to be a small step toward accepting my new identity. But identity does not change with a name. Nearly two years after Harold's death, I woke up one morning and realized that I was having an identity crisis. I eventually concluded that finding a new identity is a major task after the death of a spouse.

I was not alone. In the Living Well study, 19 percent of the people who responded to the question "What would you say is the major task or agenda of grief following the death of a spouse?" named identity issues—the second most frequently mentioned task of grief.

After being widowed for more than three years, I realized that part of the new identity that I had taken on would be temporary. I was a student, and much as I loved that role, I didn't think I would be a student forever. In 1999 I had suddenly moved from wife to widow. Now, in my fourth year of widowhood I was moving from widow to woman. I would remain a widow unless I remarried, but widow would not continue to be my primary identity. Wife to widow to woman. I was keenly aware of that transformation occurring within me.

Something else was also growing within me—a call to pastoral ministry. My call to some kind of ministry had been confirmed on 9/11, but it was not clear what kind of ministry it would be. I considered chaplaincy work, hospice work, and other types of assignments, all the while dancing around the call to pastoral ministry.

Boldness to name the call came during Pastors Week at AMBS in January 2004. During one of the sessions, my mind wandered and I suddenly had the strong feeling that it was time to take off my wedding ring. I had moved my ring to my right hand about eighteen months after Harold's death (when I realized I no longer felt married to Harold), and near the end of 2003 (four years after his death) I had thought it might soon be time to take it off. But I had not considered where or when I would do so. But there in the AMBS chapel on that January day, I knew it was the right time. I slipped off my ring and put it in my pocket.

My mind went back to thinking about a call to pastoral ministry. Two hours later, during the women pastors luncheon, I knew it was time to publicly acknowledge that I was embracing a call to pastoral ministry. During the sharing time I spoke into the microphone words of acceptance of my call. I added that I had been widowed and had removed my wedding ring two hours earlier. I said that I did not know if that was related to my new level of embracing ministry, but the two were occurring simultaneously. Then I heard myself say that I was no longer a widow—at least not in the way I had been during the previous four years. The group applauded and I sat down, not quite believing I had really said that.

No longer a widow? I had read those words four years earlier in Katie Funk Wiebe's book *Alone: A Search for Joy*. In the prologue she writes about speaking to a group of widows many years after her husband had died.

> You had told them you weren't a widow anymore. Not boastingly, just a matter-of-fact statement. The idea had come to you as you were speaking, but it had been forming a long time. You were a widow once. You thought the season of grief would never end. But it did. Widowhood didn't come to a brake-screeching halt, but slowly faded as a new person developed in you who had a clearer understanding of life and how God deals with human beings, especially those who suffer. You had told them you had been single, then married and widowed, and now were single again.[40]

I did not think I would say those words myself, at least not for a long time. But I had indeed spoken them. After lunch I went to the library to journal. As I began writing I nearly gasped. It had not occurred to me until then that I had removed my wedding ring in the same place where Harold had put it on my finger thirty-two years earlier. So in some ways I had come full circle. I left that day with joy and expectation, not knowing what would be next for me, but confident that God was leading me and that in due time next steps would be clear.

The new identity I am finding and the transformation I am experiencing is not a move from voicelessness, but it is a move from limited confidence to hearing and trusting my inner voice; from cautious and timid expressions to finding my voice; from being conflicted about life around me to being able to separate and connect the voices, to "integrating the voices." Loder writes that these processes describe "the redemption of the human spirit: the power to create and compose one's world in one's own terms."[41] The development of identity from a theological perspective includes the notion of transformation.

> Transformation is the pattern in cosmological events that redirects the course of entropy in open systems. . . .

However, the supreme transformation, which includes but transforms all these transformations of creation and the human spirit, is the transforming power of the Creator Spirit, who is at work to transform and redeem all of God's creation. This is the grand, irreversible theological figure-ground shift in which our entire developing life, the whole of the life span, the totality of one's own existence, moves into the background, and the Creator Spirit becomes the central figure, the definitive reality. The human spirit in all its proximate transformations is now ultimately grounded as spirit in God's Spirit.[42]

Loder's powerful illumination can help us to grasp a bit of understanding of how our spirit and God's Spirit work together. It is an invitation to continue on a journey of self-discovery.

Discovering who we are is not easy. Silence is necessary to hear what is within, and most of us live in a very noisy world. When we suffer loss, we often develop new priorities and learn to tune out some of the noise. If we can stay with the silence and listen to what is within, we can come to new depths of understanding of who we truly are. We have each been uniquely created in the image of God with a purpose.

Responding to God while discerning and living out that purpose takes us to new levels of meaning in life and greater joy in living. The invitation is to wait, to pay attention, to reflect on the events of our lives, and to trust that God, who loves us more than we can imagine, opens paths for us. We then emerge with new or clearer identities and new opportunities to live well.

Part 2

Sexuality

—4—

Living Well Beyond
the Crisis

Our mind's desire is to know,
to understand;
but our heart's desire is intimacy,
to be known, to be understood.
To see God with our minds would be to know God,
to understand God;
but to see God with our hearts
would be to have a sense of being known by God,
of being understood by God.
—John S. Dunne[1]

I must conquer my loneliness alone.

Two halves have little choice but to join;
and yes, they do make a whole.

But two wholes when they coincide . . .
that is beauty.
—Peter McWilliams[2]

Many resources are available for widowed people today,
from both secular and Christian sources. I have read or
reviewed dozens of books and have found many quite help-

ful in dealing with the concerns of the first year or two after the death of a loved one. However, issues that widowed people face beyond the initial years are seldom addressed. These include questions about identity, friendships, sexuality, and in some cases new romantic relationships and another marriage. Part of what led me to this project was the fact that there seemed to be so little written on these topics.

C. S. Lewis suggested how to live well while mourning the death of a spouse when he referred to bereavement as another stage of marriage. He said that just as the honeymoon follows the wedding, so bereavement follows the years of marriage for one of the partners. The invitation is to live "well and faithfully" through this stage of the marriage also, accepting the pain as a necessary part. "We don't want to escape [the pain] at the price of desertion or divorce," Lewis wrote. "Killing the dead a second time."[3]

There are many dimensions to living well and faithfully after the death of a husband or wife. To live well we need friendships. To be sure, we need relationships to live; we were created because of God's passionate desire for relationship with humanity. God created us for relationship with God. In fact, the Christian God *is* a relationship—the Trinity that is three aspects of God interrelating. Created as we are in God's image, we need relationships with God and with others. Indeed, it is in relationships that we learn to love, and it is love that gives meaning to life.[4]

Relationships Old and New

A person who has no friends may exist, but hardly lives. Rather, that person exists in the process of dying. There is dramatic evidence of this in babies who fail to thrive when they have inadequate human contact. It is well documented and acknowledged that human babies as well as babies of other mammals need parent or surrogate-parent interaction to stay alive. It is not so well recognized that this phenomenon continues throughout life.[5] In his essay, "The Gift and Intimacy," Willard Krabill writes, "Intimacy is not only desirable; it is also a real need for everyone at every age."[6]

Basic to growing and thriving is having friends who will be mirrors for us along our journey. As is true of many things in life, people often do not recognize the importance of friends until they are taken away. When one's best friend dies, the loss is huge. If the best friend was also one's lover, roommate, and daily companion, the loss may feel devastating. If, in addition, the deceased was one's breadwinner and co-parent, the loss may seem insurmountable.

The intimacy that exists and grows in good marriages is a treasure like no other, and it cannot be replaced. Intimacy may develop in other relationships, but that which was lost will not be replaced. Romantic relationships and marriage after the death of a spouse will be addressed later; friendships outside of marriage will be considered first.

Friendships

The psalmists, mystics, and contemplatives describe in various ways a longing for God within the souls of all people. In *Gate of the Temple*, Richard Rohr describes this desire as longing for union. All our lives we long for union with the other, whether God or human. We need human relationships so that we can know God. Rohr says that relationships can be sacraments, for through the physical we come to God. We cannot know the love of God unless we know the love of another human.

Friends are important and extremely significant because they help to shape who we are and who we become. Friendships are all the more important when one's spouse dies. Those who have a community to surround them at the time of the death are fortunate indeed. For friends to walk with a bereaved person in the early days after the death is crucial; to be sure, many people usually surround the bereaved at such a time.

Although there are many anecdotal stories of how widowed people experience friendships, in my research I found no studies that looked at the question of friendships following spousal death. In the Living Well study, 86 percent of the respondents said either longtime friends or church-family members, or both, were their most important support after their spouse died. Though supportive family was most frequently identified as important, friends or church members were almost as important. Thirty percent indicated that other widowed people gave important support as well.[7]

Because widowed people repeatedly report that many former friends, especially couples, do not remain supportive after the initial period following a spouse's death, the Living Well study asked about relationships with "couple friends" who were friends before the spouse's death. Of those who responded, 37 percent said *all* of their "couple friends" stood by them and 40 percent said *most* of their "couple friends" stood by them. There was not a statistically significant difference between the way women and men perceived these friendships. The population in my survey seemed to have unusually strong bases of support, possibly because in most cases they were members of a supportive faith community. However, the smaller percentages of people who felt rejected and hurt must not be ignored. Twenty-two percent said only some or none of their "couple friends" stood by them.[8]

Asking why the widowed person thought few friends stood by after the death elicited responses such as "They didn't know what to say," "They don't know how to include a single," and "Because of their own hurt." Other respondents thought that former friends made unwarranted assumptions, for example, assuming that a widow was "after" another's husband or that a widowed person would not want to spend time with married people. As a result of not being included with couples, some widowed people identified feeling alone or left out, which added to the sense of loss. Others chose to avoid spending time with groups of couples. One respondent said, regarding those who feel awkward around a widowed person, "I feel little compassion for their quandary."

On the positive side, the people who said all their couple friends stood by them gave reasons such as the strength of the friendship, things shared in common, and deliberate effort on the part of the widowed person. One respondent wrote, "They respected each of us as individuals as well as a couple." Another responded, "I said 'yes' to invitations even when I knew the evening would be difficult emotionally. I also would try to be 'fun' to be with. In the first several months I would 'pretend' sometimes."

As a result of these sustained relationships, people described feeling blessed, loved, or supported. Others expressed feeling included, respected, valued, grateful, normal, protected, safe, comforted, strengthened, or encouraged.

There were some "yes, but . . ." responses to the question about "couple friends." One example is, "They have stood beside me in that they are available *if* I ask for help. As far as inviting me to gatherings of couples, *no*, they have not stood beside me. I really miss doing things together as couples."

Regarding relationships with single friends, the differences between men and women are evident. Close to half of widows had more single friends than while they were married, and nearly half of those new friends were also widowed women. About one fourth of widowers had more single friends than before, and only a few of them were also widowed and nearly all of those were women.

When asked about *new* friendships in general, the differences between men and women were not as distinct. Descriptions of the new friends are in chart 2.

Chart 2

NEW FRIENDS	# of women	% of women	# of men	% of men
Widowed	61	60%	15	44%
Never married	16	17%	2	6%
Divorced	24	26%	7	21%
Close to my age	38	41%	11	32%
Of all age groups	46	50%	19	56%
From my church	38	41%	26	76%
From my work setting	25	27%	1	3%
From a grief group	17	18%	2	6%
Married, both genders	41	45%	18	53%
Married, same gender	6	7%	0	0%
Married, other gender	1	1%	1	3%

Responses to the question about relating to single friends of the other gender indicated that women are much more cautious than men, but for both men and women, the reason for the caution was not wanting to give "the wrong impression." Numerous widowed women (from the questionnaire and in other contexts) talked about missing male friendship.[9] One woman in her fifties said that her former male friends were really her husband's friends more than her own. As a result, she felt surrounded by only females, which she felt was mostly good, but "sometimes I just miss men." Another in her sixties wrote, "I need single male friends and seek them out."

This deficiency of other-gender friendships was described in various ways. One widow in her forties referred to needing to pay all the men who help her: her attorney, her psychotherapist, and various service providers. In one sense she even pays her pastor. She said,

"I don't want to get married again—at least not now—but I would like to have a male friend so I can hear a male perspective on things in life." Furthermore, the man needs to be single so that the friendship is not complicated by his wife. Another woman, who had remarried, said, "I missed male input. I remember wanting male relationships, not for romance, but just to be with them. It made me feel more complete."

One widower more than eighty years old remarked that he seeks out female friends. He said it may be because he misses characteristics of his late wife that he sees in these friends. This would be consistent with ideas from two contemporary contemplative Christians, Richard Rohr and Richard Foster. Rohr says that our sexuality keeps reminding us of how incomplete we are. The Latin root of the word for "sex" is to be "cut off." We long for union, the meeting of opposites, which is ultimately met in union with God. An intimate friendship can meet some of our needs for union, and it does not have to be sexual. In fact, the faith of the religious celibate asserts that it is possible to "meet the opposite without possession."[10]

Foster refers to human beings as "the apex of God's creation."[11] We know from Genesis that God created us in the image of God, *imago Dei*. And we were created *male and female*. Both our maleness and femaleness reflect the image of God. Foster credits Karl Barth as the first major theologian to illuminate

> the implications of this tremendous confession of Scripture that human sexuality is grounded in the *imago Dei*. What [Barth] has helped us understand is that relationship is at the heart of what it means to be "in the image of God" and that the relationship between male and female is the human expression of our relationship with God.[12]

"Our human sexuality, our maleness and femaleness," continues Foster, "is at the center of our true humanity. We exist as male and female in relationship. Our sexualness, our capacity to love and be loved, is intimately related to our creation in the image of God."[13] Thus our sexuality, our desire to be intimately united with another, is grounded in the image of God. Although this union can be—and often is—genital, sexuality is far *more* than genitality, far *more* than sexual intercourse. Friendships with people of the opposite sex are very important, perhaps even necessary, for living well.

Same-sex friendships are also important. Many women in my study referred to the importance of friendships with other women. A man in his sixties wrote, "Some very meaningful male friendships developed, but with a second marriage they have not been sustained." Although many needs for intimacy can be met in same-sex friendships, most people are interested in and seek intimacy with people of the opposite sex.

New Attractions

One of the great dilemmas regarding relationships with the opposite sex after losing a spouse is that many people begin to feel sexual attractions while they are still in the midst of grief, before they are ready for another relationship.[14] In many cases this happens long before family members, especially children, are ready for the bereaved person to move into another relationship. To try to determine the typical range of timing of new attractions, the Living Well questionnaire asked, "If you have experienced an attraction to or interest in a person(s) of the opposite gender, when did it occur in relation to the death of your late spouse?"

Fifty-one percent of the women who responded to the *questionnaire* indicated that they were attracted to a man after being widowed, and 87 percent of men were attracted to a woman.[15] Of the people who responded to this *specific question*, 79 percent of women and 93 percent of men indicated they experienced an attraction to a person of the opposite sex. Information about the timing of these attractions for the 110 people who responded to the question is presented in chart 3.

Chart 3

ATTRACTIONS NOTED	# people	% people	# women	% women	# men	% men
within first 3 mo.	11	12%	3	5.5%	8	21%
3 to 6 months	13	14%	5	9%	8	21%
6 to 9 months	13	14%	6	11%	7	18%
9 to 12 months	9	10%	4	7%	5	13%
12 to 18 months	13	14%	9	16.5%	4	10%
18 to 24 months	5	5%	3	5.5%	2	5%
2 to 3 years	13	14%	11	20%	2	5%
3 to 4 years	5	5%	4	7%	1	2.5%
5 years	5	5%	3	5.5%	2	5%
9 to 10 years	3	3%	3	5.5%	0	0
Other –unspecified	3	3%	3	5.5%	0	0
TOTALS with attractions	93	84.5%	54	79%	39	93%
No attractions	17	15.5%	14	21%	3	7%
TOTAL answers to this question	110		68		42	

A significant difference between men's and women's attractions was in the timing of when they first occurred. Chart 3 demonstrates that men tend to note an attraction to women (or at least admitted to it) sooner after spousal death than do women. While 73 percent of widowers indicated they were attracted to a woman within the first year after the death, less than half (32.5 percent) of women indicated they were attracted to a man during the first year.

New Relationships

Many people whose partners die are encouraged sooner or later to consider the possibility of new romantic relationships. Often others offer such encouragement before the bereaved person is ready for another relationship. On the other hand, as noted above, some bereaved people are interested in a new relationship before family members are "ready" for them to become involved with someone else, and perhaps before they are really "ready" themselves. But what does it mean to be "ready"? One woman told this story:

> The night my husband died, my brother who had been widowed several years earlier stayed up late with me. We talked about many things. Both of our spouses had died unexpectedly leaving us with young children and we had much in common. He had remarried, and at one point he said I would probably marry again. I said I couldn't even think about that, but then I did think about it for a moment and a man came to my mind. Just as quickly I put him out of my mind and didn't think about him again for several weeks. Four months later I found I was thinking about him a lot, and by six months I was quite infatuated with him. This startled me because I was still clearly grieving my husband's death. Fortunately I had an excellent counselor in whom I confided these feelings. She listened and said, "You're not ready for another relationship." I agreed that I was not, but eagerly asked her when I would be. She had a very wise response: "When you don't need it."

Some who get involved with another person soon after the death of a spouse eventually recognize that it was out of neediness that they sought a new relationship. Extra challenges will likely be present in a relationship if it develops because of neediness rather than the strengths of the partners. These challenges, in addition to the objections of children whose widowed parents enter new relationships, and the dilemmas that friends and pastors face when a recently widowed person is eager to marry again, prompt questions. More than half the marriages of widowed people who remarry within the first two years after spousal death end in divorce.[16]

One thoughtful, formerly widowed person suggested that it is best to figure out how to live with empty spaces in your life. Perhaps a person is in a state of being ready for another relationship when he or she has gone on with life and has invested in new interests other than a romantic relationship—not sitting around waiting for, or out desperately *searching* for, a new companion. The above person added, "To have a good enduring relationship, people need to have more in common than grief; one should ask what kind of a life you want and look for someone who will share that with you."

The Living Well study asked about new relationships. Forty-nine percent of the respondents said they had dated/courted/spent time with a person of the opposite sex.[17] Of these, 36 percent of the women and 82 percent of the men said they have dated. The time these relationships began in relation to the death of the spouse is detailed in chart 4.

Chart 4

DATING RELATIONSHIPS EXPERIENCED	# people	% people	# women	% women	# men	% men
within first 3 mo.	6	8%	1	2.5%	5	13.5%
3 to 6 months	8	10.5%	1	2.5%	7	19%
6 to 9 months	8	10.5%	2	5%	6	16%
9 to 12 months	7	9%	2	5%	5	13.5%
12 to 18 months	12	16%	6	16%	6	16%
18 to 24 months	9	12%	7	18.5%	2	5%
2 to 3 years	15	20%	12	31.5%	3	8%
3 to 4 years	5	7%	4	10.5%	1	2.5%
5 years	5	7%	3	8%	2	5%
TOTALS with relationships	75		38		37	

Men began dating much more quickly than women, with the majority (62 percent) of men who dated beginning within the first year after their spouse's death. By contrast, only 15 percent of women dated within the first year afterward. Fifty percent of women waited until more than two years had passed before dating.

The reasons for these significant differences were not part of this study. There are numerous theories about the differences in the way men and women grieve, some of them spelled out in a book by Elizabeth Levang.[18] One respondent to the questionnaire said she thought women cope with widowhood better than men, partly because women can more easily talk and share feelings.

Another theory that a fellow researcher has come across is that men tend to have greater sexual desires during times of transition than at ordinary times. In her work with couples in transition she has found this to be true. It is the opposite for women; they tend to desire less sexual activity during transitions than they typically do. Indeed, most widowed people face numerous transitions.

It is observed in the Living Well study that the differences in the percentages of men versus women who eventually date after the death of a spouse is not because of huge differences between men and women in feeling attractions to people of the opposite sex.[19] As noted above, 79 percent of the women who responded to the question indicated that they were attracted to men after being widowed, and 93 percent of the men were attracted to women, whereas only 36 percent of the women and 82 percent of the men said they had dated.

It is interesting to note the timing patterns of experiencing an attraction versus actually beginning to date. Chart 5 compares the timing of first feeling attractions and of actually dating for those who indicated having these experiences.

Chart 5

FIRST ATTRACTIONS VS. FIRST DATING	Women with attractions	Women who dated	Men with attractions	Men who dated
Within first year	33%	16%	72%	62%
Between 1 and 2 years	22%	34%	15%	22%
2 years or longer	39% [20]	50%	13%	16%

An additional obvious reason for differences in dating statistics between men and women is the fact that there are far more widowed women than men. This is related to women having a longer life expectancy and being more likely to marry men older than themselves. The 2000 U.S. census indicated that of the 10.3 million widowed people in 1999, 82 percent were women and 18 percent were men.[21]

Some respondents shared stories about dating and marriage after being widowed. Respondent Reuben reported on a six-month relationship during his fifth year of widowhood:

Although there was a mutual agreement to end the relationship and we remained friends, there was a lot of pain for me in the loss. Since a significant time had passed since the death of my spouse, I didn't think I was trying to replace my spouse in the new relationship, but yet I wondered, because with the new loss I experienced deep pain that reminded me of how I felt after my spouse died, and because I again felt the loss of my spouse— more intensely than I had felt for a long time. The good news is that I bounced back more quickly. I think there are a number of reasons: six months is a very short time compared with many years of marriage; there was no commitment in this new relationship; and perhaps most importantly, I had experienced a profound loss in the death of my spouse and had survived that. I had feelings of despair and anger and intense sadness in relation to the new loss, but I knew that in time I would find a way to move on again. The amazing thing was that even in the midst of the pain, I did not regret having been in the relationship. It was lovely while it lasted, and the joy in being together outweighed the pain when it ended. And perhaps even more amazing is that I am open to another loving relationship. Love *is* worth the risk of losing!

Another respondent wrote,

> Recently a handsome widowed man asked me to go out to eat. I refused. I do not wish to remarry because of problems it could cause with my children. I have been very cautious because I have observed some widowed friends who have remarried to the regret of their friends and themselves. I know of an elderly widow who remarried and died on the night of their wedding. A widower had a similar experience. A friend remarried at ninety-plus and died a year later.

Many people said they had no regrets about relationships in which they had been involved, but some people who remarried named regrets. One person in a continuing relationship said, "I was very vulnerable in dating so soon and mistook physical affection for love." A woman whose second marriage ended in divorce said, "I so wished I had listened to my instincts and not married him. We were not married long until I saw he was attracted to other women and then found out he was having an affair." Another respondent said, "I regret becoming physically involved too early." Noteworthy is that many who named regrets referred to moving into new relationships too quickly.

Respondents were invited to share what they had learned from dating experiences and marriage, and many offered reflections and advice. Opinions depended on their perspective. One man in his forties said he would not date if he were in his sixties. But one woman responded that she was surprised by the intensity of the sexual feelings she and her new husband both experience, as they are in their sixties. Was the forty-something man unable to imagine that he could still have interest in and capacity for sex when he was sixty?

Fifty-eight people answered this question: "What would you do differently if you were starting over in the dating process or what advice would you give (regarding dating) to a recently widowed person?" Fifty people offered advice, most of them remarried, engaged, or in a continuing relationship. Of these, 48 percent said in various ways, "Take your time!" That advice is so consistent that it should not be ignored. It comes from people who "have been there," who know the great pain that comes with the death of a spouse and of the loneliness that follows. They know the feelings of attraction to another person, but they also know the pain of living with decisions that were made too quickly or for the wrong reasons.

Notably, there was not agreement on the timing of involving children in meeting a new potential partner, which illustrates that situations vary greatly.

Many responses refer to loneliness as a reason for beginning a new romantic relationship. The lines from Peter McWilliams that opened this chapter are worth recalling. He refers to conquering loneliness alone, so that one can become not a "half person" joining another half, but a whole person who may join another whole.[22] While conquering loneliness requires solitary work, the best outcome occurs when the work is done with the awareness of God's presence and within a supportive community.

Marriage After Widowhood

Many people who responded to the Living Well study entered into new relationships following the death of their spouse. About a third who responded to the questionnaire remarried. Twenty-two percent of the women remarried and 62 percent of the men had married again. Chart 6 reports this data according to the length of time after the respondent was widowed.

Chart 6

REMARRIAGE	Total	%[23]	Women	%	Men	%
Number of respondents who remarried[24]	51	33.5%	23	22%	28	62%
Number widowed within previous year who remarried	1	9%	0	0	1	100%
Number widowed 1 to 2 years earlier who remarried	0	0	0	0	0	0
Number widowed 2 to 3 years earlier who remarried	1	8%	1	9%	0	0
Number widowed 3 to 4 years earlier who remarried	5	31%	3	21%	2	100%
Number widowed 4 to 5 years earlier who remarried	3	50%	1	25%	2	75%
Number widowed 5 to 10 years earlier who remarried	11	26%	4	10.5%	7	47%
Number widowed 10 to 20 years earlier who remarried	15	43%	9	32%	6	86%
Number widowed more than 20 years earlier who remarried	14	70%	5	45%	9	100%

Respondents identified ways second marriages differed from the first. Some noted that the second marriage was more compatible or had more physical intimacy. One wrote, "We never take a day for granted. We talk together more than in our first marriages." Another described the second marriage as "more peaceful; less stressful, more like living with a good friend." Some differences brought tension. "Communication is a major challenge," one person stated. "We come with years of set patterns, and don't 'grow up' together in second marriage. [We have] two sets of children with nothing in common."

Forty-four of the married respondents answered the question, "In light of your own experience, what advice regarding marriage would you give to widowed people who have not remarried?" The following advice stands out:

- Although a second marriage can be good, single-ness can also be a good way to live and a time to experience new things and grow.
- If you do remarry, take some special precautions such as premarital counseling and a prenuptial agreement.
- Take plenty of time to begin and process new rela-tionships.

Thirty-four percent of those who answered this question advised taking plenty of time. This confirms what was noted above, that experienced people say taking time is very important.

Some sort of attachment to a deceased spouse usually continues into a second marriage. This is confirmed by references to remarriage after widowhood in psychological and sociological academic literature. One significant essay refers to the triadic relationship (or two interlocking triads in cases where both partners had been widowed) that exists in remarriage of widowed people.[25] It is noted that most widowed people maintain meaningful ties with the deceased and the life they had during those marriages. It is concluded that "a prolonged attachment to a deceased spouse, even after remarriage, is timeless. As such it is gen-erally neither pathological nor maladaptive."[26] This is an important consideration for anyone marrying a widowed person.

Spousal sanctification—revering the deceased spouse as sacred, remembering only the positive things about him or her—was not mentioned specifically (and barely noted) by any of my respondents, but it is referred to in other research. One study reported that divorced men did not want to date widows because they could not compete with the "perfection" of the deceased husband.[27] This phenomenon would probably be more likely to show up in a study of people who were not widowed themselves, but married someone who had been widowed.[28]

The Living Well study did not focus on the joys of new relationships following widowhood, but some of the joy and enthusiasm came through. Respondent Paula was widowed when she had young children and married again in her seventies after forty years of widowhood. She said that dating at seventy was just as exciting as at sixteen.

A summary of remarriage following spousal death came from Ben, who wrote six years after the death of his first wife and approximately three years after being married to his second: "The challenge of walking on into new relational, personal, and geographic territory demands a psychological venture offering fear and rich rewards. It's an act of immense faith in yourself, others, and God. It's been tough! It's been beautiful. It's worth it!"

Attitudes Regarding Sexuality

Sexuality is at the heart of an interest in new relationships following spousal death. Ronald Rolheiser presents a spirituality of sexuality: "A mature sexuality is when a person looks at what he or she has helped create, swells in a delight that breaks the prison of his or her selfishness, and feels as God feels when God looks at creation."[29] As noted above, from the root of the word *sex* comes the idea that sexuality is an awareness of having been cut off. We are cut off when we are born, and being cut off is experienced as very painful—an aching loneliness and an irrational longing, but also a great energy. In fact, our sexuality is "the greatest energy of all inside us."[30] Of course sexuality is far more than genital behavior, finding a lover, or even finding a friend. "It is about overcoming separateness by giving life and blessing it," Rolheiser says. "Thus in its maturity, sexuality is about giving oneself over to community, friendship, family, service, creativity, humor, delight, and martyrdom so that, with God, we can help bring life into the world."[31]

Jesus had a high view of sexuality as is illustrated in Matthew 19:4-6. His words to the Pharisees were, "Have you not read that the one who made them at the beginning 'made them male and female. . . . For this reason a man shall leave his father and mother and be joined to his wife, and the two shall become one flesh'? So they are no longer two, but one flesh."

Foster points out that "in these words of Jesus we encounter the great mystery of the life-uniting reality of 'one flesh.' There is a merger of two that, without destroying individuality, produces unity."[32] Furthermore, this unity is a result of God's activity, according to Donald Goergon.[33] This is clearly mystery! Mary and Robert Joyce describe this as "Two persons in one flesh, three persons in one divine reality, related mysteries of similar profundity and splendor."[34]

Keith Clark broadly defines human sexuality as "all those activities which stem from or lead to the gratification of my biological urges and emotional drives and which stem from and lead to the fulfillment of my personal need for intimacy."[35] James Nelson says that sexuality "is our way of being in the world as bodyselves who are gendered biologically and socially, who have varying sexual orientations, who have the capacity for sensuousness, who have the need for intimacy, who have varied and often conflicting feelings about what it means to be bodied."[36]

Understanding human growth and spiritual development helps in understanding sexuality. Erik Erikson's description of the stage of generativity sheds light on the sexuality of mature adults. In this stage, adults are concerned with establishing and guiding the next generation, with making a contribution to the world, and with participating in activities that lead to a sense of vitality.[37] Many adults in their seventies, eighties, and even nineties have a keen sense of vitality that includes an alert sexuality.

Anne Hershberger and Willard Krabill put it well: "Our sexuality is that pervasive essence of our personality that forever and every time defines us first as humans and second as males or females." They emphasize that sexuality is to be celebrated. "Sexuality is for rejoicing; . . . How beautiful that sexuality was created as a dimension of God's highest creation."[38] Encountering the mystery in our sexuality and in our sexual encounters may be like walking through an enchanting long dark tunnel with the mystery illuminating the path. The light at the end of the tunnel is unseen at times, but engaging with the mystery sheds light on each step.

Intimacy in Marriage

In an effort to sort through the layers of marital intimacy and bring into focus the aspects of a spouse's absence that are most difficult, the Living Well study asked, "What did you miss most about your spouse in the first months after the death?" The following options were offered, with respondents asked to rate them starting with 1 as most missed.

___ my spouse's overall companionship
___ my spouse's physical presence
___ our emotional intimacy
___ our sexual intimacy
___ our physical (but not necessarily sexual) intimacy
___ other

Sixty-eight percent rated "my spouse's overall companionship" as what they missed most. Eighteen percent rated "my spouse's physical presence" as number one.

Only one person rated "our sexual intimacy" as number one.[39] Six people (two women and four men) rated "our sexual intimacy" as the number two thing missed most.

Of the people who checked items in this question, fifty-seven percent did *not* check "our sexual intimacy" as something that was missed. Of those people, 63 were women, 23 were men.

The high number who said they did not miss sexual intimacy might be surprising, even keeping in mind that the question asked about the early months after spousal death. This does not necessarily mean that all who answered the question did not miss sexual intimacy; a few checked only one item, perhaps not understanding that they could check more than one.[40]

It is interesting to look at these responses beside the replies to a question about sexual longings. Later in this chapter we will note that 37 percent of the people who answered the question about sexual longings said that they have or had increased sexual desire after the death; they had missed sexual intimacy or still had sexual interests. An explanation for what might at first seem a discrepancy may be that although many people missed sexual intimacy, the spouse's overall companionship, physical presence, and emotional intimacy were missed even more.

Spirituality and Sexuality

A grief journey is inevitably and inescapably a spiritual journey. The questions with which one struggles following the death of a loved one are spiritual issues. When it is a spouse who has died, sexuality is involved, and our spirituality and sexuality are very closely connected. Our longing for God and our longing for union with another human are similar, and they can be confused. Sources differ regarding how to interpret such connections. On one hand, in *Gate of the Temple: Spirituality and Sexuality*, Rohr articulates the similarities in these longings. He affirms that spirituality and sexuality are two sides of the same coin.[41] On the other hand, Loder claims that "sexuality is a proximate and deficient longing for a deeper intimacy that only the spiritual life can provide."[42]

The spiritual journey following the death of a spouse is different from the journey following most other losses, in part because of the sexual connection spouses have. It is no wonder that being widowed results in an enormous emptiness, especially for one who feels cut off from God, which many bereaved people do for at least a time. Losing the opportunity for sexual intimacy at the same time as feeling distant from God is huge. But a gift in the loss of sexual expression with one's spouse is the opportunity to re-evaluate the inner longing and emptiness that comes with widowhood.

One may discover that some of the innate inner longing for God was partially fulfilled in the sexual intimacy one experienced with a spouse. A sexual experience can never replace the longing for God, but it is possible for a good sexual relationship to partially mask the longing for God, as is illustrated in the story of Mari in chapter 3. In addition, Goergen points out that it is "easy to confuse the need for genital sex with the need for sexual identity, the need for self-acceptance, or the need for closeness."[43]

While muddling in the inner darkness of grief and walking in the valley of the shadow of death, a widowed person can come to more clearly understand those inner longings and more surely know which of the longings can be fulfilled in an intimate human relationship and which can be satisfied only in relationship to God. Because of this, the death of a spouse is one of the most profound opportunities for spiritual growth that most people will ever encounter.

Why did God create us as sexual beings? Is it because through our sexuality we recognize our desperate isolation as individuals and our vital need for intimacy? It *is* through our sexuality that we are drawn to another, and in learning to love and give of ourselves to another, we learn that love is much more than an interest in another person. The most important commandments are to love God and to love others. Perhaps the most important thing in life is that we become loving people, that we deepen our capacity to love and to be loved. Thus we are drawn into community, because our need for intimacy is not fulfilled in a relationship with *only* a significant other, and our one-to-one intimate relationships need a community in which to flourish.

Death, Sex, and Spirituality

The connections between spirituality and sexuality are articulated by many theologians and spiritual writers, including Foster, Loder, Joyce and Joyce, Rohr, and Rolheiser. However, Loder adds death to the discussion: "Sex, death, and spirituality are deeply intertwined. The bottom line is that sex is simply nature's answer to death. In itself, sex has no other meaning. It is the human spirit that gives sex its meaning . . . but in no case can sexuality be adequately understood apart from death."[44] To be sure, on one fundamental level, sexuality, and specifically sexual intercourse, is the answer to death in that it continues the propagation of the species. On another level, in sexual intercourse one becomes vulnerable, completely giving oneself (even if just for a moment) to the other. In a sense, the self is momentarily obliterated during a sexual orgasm.

Indeed, it has been said that a sexual orgasm is a small death. Does it follow then that death is the ultimate orgasm? If so, is that why widowed people who have "tasted death"—in the death of the spouse—long for an additional "taste of death" in another sexual relationship? And if that is so, is it because there is so little understanding of death, and in an orgasm there is the potential of coming to greater insights about death? Could this possibly be an answer to the widowed person who masturbates to what seems to be an excess and who struggles for some understanding? Or a partial explanation as to why many people have an interest in and/or seek new sexual relationships soon after the death of a spouse? In *Eros in Mourning,* Henry Staten states,

> Mourning is the horizon of all desire. . . . It is necessary to transpose the problematic of desire into the key of mourning. As soon as desire is . . . felt by a mortal being for a mortal being, eros . . . will always be to some degree agitated by the anticipation of loss—an anticipa-

tion that operates even with regard to what is not yet possessed."[45]

Another striking statement from literature that speaks of sex, death, and spirituality comes in "Praying Mantis," a poem by Japanese Mennonite poet, Yorifumi Yaguchi in which he describes a male praying mantis being eaten by his female. He imagines the male's "wild shout of ecstasy as his wife ate him" and his joy that "seemed to increase the more his body was violently bitten along." Later Yaguchi wondered "if his swallowed body was digested or . . . still praying in her."[46]

For many people these ideas raise more questions rather than provide answers. However, more study of the interrelationships of death, sexuality, and spirituality could lead to greater understandings in all three fields and particularly to a better grasp of living well after the death of a spouse.

More fully comprehending death, sexuality, and spirituality can also help prepare one to live a celibate life. However, before addressing the issue of celibacy we will reflect on some of the Christian roots of common attitudes regarding sexuality.

Augustine and Pelagius

Although St. Augustine of Hippo (354-430) is considered one of the greatest theologians in western Christianity, there is general agreement that part of the negativity and shame with which sexuality has been regarded by the Christian church is rooted in his negativity toward sex. He held that "intercourse for the purpose of generation (procreation) has no fault attached to it, but for the purpose of satisfying concupiscence (sexual desire), provided with a spouse, because of the marriage fidelity, it is a venial (forgivable) sin; adultery or fornication, however, is a mortal sin."[47] Rather than being viewed as a wholesome, natural part of human personality and expression, sexuality was considered a distorted, shameful aspect of humanity.

J. Philip Newell compares the teachings of Augustine

and Pelagius. A late fourth-century contemporary of Augustine, Pelagius, the first significant British theologian, went to Rome promoting a "strong sense of the goodness of creation, in which the life of God can be glimpsed."[48] He was eventually excommunicated from the church due in part to the efforts of Augustine, who considered the Pelagius teachings to be heresy.

Most controversial was Pelagius' teaching that every child is conceived and born in the image of God. Augustine, and the Roman church in general, emphasized the evil and unrighteousness in humanity. The generalized appraisal of Augustine's writings is that he believed that the "human child is born depraved and humanity's sinful nature has been sexually transmitted from one generation to the next . . . [and] that from conception and birth we lack the image of God until it is restored in the sacrament of baptism."[49] Newell says that "the perspective conveyed by Pelagius on the other hand, is that to look into the face of a newborn is to look at the image of God; he maintained that creation is essentially good and that the sexual dimension of procreation is God-given."[50] In some circles, especially those influenced by Celtic spirituality, it is held that the Pelagian view of creation and sexuality is more biblical and more theologically sound than the Augustinian's. I would agree.

Goergen concurs that negativity regarding sexuality is related to Augustine's influence. He examines theology and sexuality in Genesis, in the Song of Songs, in Jesus' words in Matthew, in Paul, and in Augustine. Of these, he finds that only Augustine has a negative view of sexuality, of intercourse being only for procreation, and even with that intent, of it being somewhat tainted by sin, as he refers to "the shame which attends all sexual intercourse."[51] None of the other theologies examined consider sexuality to be exclusively for procreative activity nor do any of them object to sexual pleasure. In fact, the Song of Songs reveals a celebrative attitude toward sensual pleasure. Goergen summarizes his study with the following statements:

1. Negativity in the face of sensual pleasure is not Judaeo-Christian.
2. Sexuality is linked to fellowship and love in both Old and New Testaments.
3. Fidelity and the Kingdom of God are the setting for the New Testament discussions of sexuality, not pleasure and procreation.
4. Not only is fidelity important; so is eschatology, which is central to the New Testament.
5. Both sexual intercourse and sexual abstinence are New Testament values. Neither is the supreme Christian value. What is important is life in Christ.[52]

Goergen concludes:

> Sexuality is an indication that we are not created self-subsistent beings. We are created incomplete by ourselves, relational beings, in need of others. God does not intend us to be alone. Independence is not our goal. Love is the Christian value and sex is a gift from God that exists for the sake of this love. God's intention is not only that two become one but that someday we will all be one as Jesus and his Father are one. Sexuality is part of the totality of the divine plan.[53]

Celibacy

One of the dramatic changes for most widowed people after the death of spouse is the change from a pattern of life that included sexual activity (usually intercourse, but not always, especially in cases where the spouse was ill) to a celibate life. For many this change is dramatic, and there are few forums in which the sexuality of widowed people is addressed. For that reason, this study includes significant discussion on sexuality and particularly on celibacy.

Celibacy is defined variously as temporarily abstaining from sexual intercourse, a part of a lifelong vow to a religious calling, or a commitment to a relationship with God that will not be distracted by commitments to spouse or children. Nouwen said the best definition of celibacy is the definition of Thomas Aquinas: "a vacancy for God." Nouwen said "to be a celibate means to be empty for God, to be free and open for [God's] presence, to be available for [God's] service."[54]

> Celibacy, in its deepest sense of creating and protecting emptiness for God, is an essential part of all forms of Christian life: marriage, friendship, single life, and community life. We will never fully understand what it means to be celibate unless we recognize that celibacy is, first of all, an element, and even an essential element in the life of all Christians.[55]

Joyce and Joyce say that the grace of God and the grace of creation develop the natural gift of celibacy.

> The human person develops by absorbing his body into his powers. [One] is meant to assimilate, rather than dominate, [one's] sexuality. Simply keeping [one's] passions under control of [one's] mind is defensive and passive. [One] is meant to do something very active, . . . to receive [one's] sexuality into the depths of oneself, transforming its impulses rather than reacting against them.[56]

Joyce and Joyce go on to say that celibacy is a kind of marriage, a union with oneself that becomes an interior marriage. "This inner union is the consummation of [one's] aloneness; it is also the fulfillment of [one's] openness to the existence of all that is. In receiving the open aloneness of his being, the person receives his being-within-the-world, another kind of union."[57]

In this study, I use celibacy to mean abstaining from sexual intercourse for at least a time. It does not mean being asexual. We cannot *not* be sexual, for God created us as sexual beings. We are sexual in the broad sense of the word all of our lives. And being celibate certainly does not mean being without close relationships.[58] We need to be connected with others to know ourselves and to know God. Rohr says, "We know ourselves only in mirrors, only in relationship. . . . We wait in darkness, unaware of ourselves, living in illusions and shadows as C. S. Lewis says, 'until we have faces.'"[59]

A commitment to reserve sexual intercourse for marriage is not one that every moral person or even every

Christian makes. My study is not a critique of that. What is offered here is a discussion about managing sexual energy during a time in life when one is without a sexual partner. No responses to the Living Well study or any conclusions drawn from the literature suggest that living celibately is easy.

It is a complicated process to detach sexually from a deceased partner, perhaps more so than ending a sexual relationship with a living person. Why are the effects of the death of a spouse—an event that occurs for nearly half of all married people—so all-encompassing and so profound? Billman and Migliore summarized a piece of Freud's work:

> When a love object dies, the task of grief is to "decathect" or detach the libido from an object no longer capable of meeting one's needs, so that one may reinvest in a new object. This process of "mourning" is very demanding because the mourner rebels against the loss and is reluctant to abandon the original attachment.[60]

Most of the information about celibacy in current literature is within a religious context or for young people before marriage. This book looks at celibacy as a way of living for mature adults that is not rooted in a religious commitment and is not necessarily for a lifetime. A person may be interested in marriage but postpones or chooses not to marry for any number of reasons. It is hoped that with this information, the invitation to celibacy may become clearer and more attractive, and living celibately may become more manageable and more rewarding, whether it is for a period of time or for a lifetime.

Models for Celibate Living

One naturally thinks of religious orders when thinking of celibacy. While much can be learned from religious celibates, and indeed I benefited greatly from many writings by both male and female religious celibates, there are additional resources that help to inform the following models for living celibately.

Celibacy as heart work

The first model for living celibately that is briefly presented involves heart and spirit work. Kathleen Norris describes conversations with religious celibate women who talked with striking clarity. One prioress said, "The worst sin against celibacy is to pretend to not have any affections at all. To fall in love is celibacy at work"! The goal is not to deny affection or sexual passion, but to make a realistic assessment of celibate sexuality, for "celibacy is not a vow to repress our feelings. It is a vow to put all our feelings, acceptable or not, close to our hearts and bring them into consciousness through prayer."[61]

Celibacy as head work

A second model is presented in a small booklet by Mary Rosera Joyce, *How Can a Man and Woman be Friends?* If the model described by the Catholic prioress is heart work, this model is head work. Self-awareness is necessary for personal growth toward maturity. A young person who lacks self-knowledge and self-esteem may tend to experience sexuality as a stimulus-response reflex. This may also be true of adults who are not self-aware or are in a very vulnerable situation. Joyce says that an understanding of one's deeper sexuality, strengthened by self-esteem, will "cause the stimulus-response reflex to develop into a stimulus-reflection-response process."[62]

Reflection helps one to create or associate some meaning with the stimulus or feelings, and then make a decision about a response, rather than letting it simply emerge from the stimulus without thought or reflection. Simply put, this is using one's brain. And after all, the brain is the human being's primary sexual organ!

As one recognizes and ponders the female anima or male animus within oneself, the sexual powers, which are receptive and expressive, can become balanced and integrated, thus realizing an inward sexual union. When one becomes more comfortable with the anima and the animus, one develops the ability to relate with the self—and also to one of the opposite sex—with deep "qualities of friendship: equality, esteem, affection and value-sharing."[63]

Friendship increases sexual freedom. Joyce says that "anyone who thinks that genital intercourse is necessary to a sexual relationship, or necessary for physical, emotional, or mental health, lacks true sexual freedom. . . . Genital necessity is a result of an unbalanced sexuality within the self." But friendship is a value in itself, "not simply a means to an end."

> Repression is a way of blocking awareness of an impulse. It is a way of denying the very existence of an urge without even being aware that you are denying it. The urge or desire is buried alive inside of oneself. And burial is just what that impulse does *not* need.
>
> If, on the other hand, the person gives *immediate* expression to an impulse, he or she is also blocking what the impulse really needs: integration with consciousness. The stimulus-response or impulsive kind of expression, where a person seeks immediate gratification of an urge or desire, is simply a reverse kind of repression. The impulse is not being buried alive; it is being born dead. It has not had enough time to gestate within one's conscious life. It needs to gestate, somewhat as a child needs to do in the mother's womb before being born.
>
> In both kinds of repression—burial alive and still-birth—the natural process of human development is damaged, and the person becomes sexually retarded.
>
> The alternative to repression is expression! Not thoughtless, acting-out expression, but thoughtful acting-inward expression! Inward expression is totally positive. Repression is totally negative.
>
> By being directed inward, the outward-tending impulse is neither repressed nor suppressed. It is simply expressed—within. It is received, understood, and encouraged to develop deeper roots in human awareness.
>
> An erotic impulse actually needs and wants inward sexual expression before it is ready for outward expression. And this inward expression is the central form of sexual activity. It is the heart of true sexual freedom.[64]

Joyce says that the central process of human sexual development is inward sexual expression, turning our feelings and urges upward—letting the "impulse 'flow into our head' and find its own center there." Through reflection a person can develop a "strong and vital sense of self and a balanced, dynamic manhood or womanhood." This helps one to "see with mental eyes and touch with mental hands," allowing both eyes and hands to become less possessive and more tender. This then allows a person to develop a capacity for sexual friendship. This "connecting process could also be called the 'centering' of erotic feelings."[65] This is not sublimation in the sense that Freud and many other psychologists described sublimation, that is, as a defense mechanism.

> When we let an erotic feeling become centered in consciousness, we are not putting up a defense mechanism. We are engaging in a natural process of human development. Social pressure can encourage or discourage this process. But only self-knowledge and a quiet, loving reflection can cause this centering to occur.[66]

This process is assimilation instead of sublimation or repression. "An erotic feeling is assimilated in consciousness," Joyce writes, "not by being digested, but by being integrated with self-knowledge and esteem, and in this way being transformed while remaining itself." She goes on to acknowledge that "an erotic urge wants outward expression. But it also wants inward movement toward its own consciousness-raising center so that it can have some kind of lasting meaning in its outward expression."[67]

Joyce offers guidelines for responding to sexual desires. One can learn to receive

> erotic feelings into your mental hands, holding them gently and encouraging them to find *their* center. Don't try to manage them. This is not just a matter of self-control or of self-management. It is just a quiet self-process. Open your mind and let your erotic desires enter. Welcome them. Receive them. Feel them. Understand them. No repression is needed. . . . Touching and holding without possessing. Without manipulation. Just receiving. This is the source of tenderness.[68]

Sexual centering includes the mental work of reflecting on one's sexuality, affirming an awareness of it and integrating it into life meanings and values. It also puts a check on impulsive behavior. The mind is so important to sexuality because it is the "meaning-seeking and value-seeking force" within one's sexuality as well as within one's total self. Neither mental forces or physical forces should be repressed; "rather, they should be developed."[69]

A man is more vulnerable in his physical response to a woman, and a woman is more vulnerable in her emotional response to a man; her eroticism is more emotional than genital. Joyce explains that to respond to the impulse to be erotically possessive, one can turn the impulse inward. She describes that a woman can respond by

> not repressing it, but recognizing, affirming, and receiving the impulse into her mind and soul. She needs loving inward reflection upon herself as a person and about the man as a person. She needs to let the energy of her possessive and seductive feelings enter and energize her consciousness. This energy is needed to develop an authentically independent sense of herself. As a result, she will not feel driven to find her identity in a man. Only then will she be ready to relate with an attractive man as a person rather than as a security mechanism.[70]

By this process a couple can "have their relationship centered in their meanings and values rather than in their ownership needs."[71] This is a model that can be very beneficial for those who are celibate as well as for those who have sexual intercourse.

Self-actualization

Although not a model as such, psychological maturity and intimate nonsexual friendships can aid one in living celibately. Abraham Maslow said that the self-actualizing person (one who is self-accepting, independent, and although loving, is free from pressures to please others) is able to be celibate and still be at ease with the self and his or her sexual life. Only when accompanied by feelings of unworthiness, isolation, inferiority, or a sense of rejection by the opposite sex is celibacy problematic.

Goergen illuminates Maslow's theory, saying "It is not genital abstinence in itself but one's attitude towards it and how one experiences it that is significant."[72] Maslow had written:

> It is certainly fair to say that self-actualizing men and women tend on the whole not to seek sex for its own sake, or to be satisfied with it alone when it comes. . . . The sexual pleasures are found in their most intense and ecstatic perfection in self-actualizing people. If love is a yearning for the perfect and for complete fusion, then the orgasm as sometimes reported by self-actualizing people becomes the attainment of it. . . . In self-actualizing people the orgasm is simultaneously more important and less important than in average people. It is often a profound and almost mystical experience, and yet the absence of sexuality is more easily tolerated by these people. This is not a paradox or a contradiction. It follows from dynamic motivation theory. Loving at a higher need level makes the lower needs and their frustrations and satisfactions less important, less central, more easily neglected. But it also makes them more wholeheartedly enjoyed when gratified. . . . These people do not *need* sensuality; they simply enjoy it when it occurs.[73]

This helps to put the sexual desires of a self-actualizing person in perspective. The mature person is "less driven to love affairs, yet free to admit of and talk about his or her sexual attractions for other people." It is easy to confuse sexual desire and the need for intimacy. Maslow describes the higher need in people to be the need for intimacy. A sexual desire may "represent the need for intimacy," but if intimacy needs are met and satisfied in other ways, the "need" for physiological genital experience is lessened.[74] As noted earlier, intimacy needs can certainly be met without sexual intercourse.

Living with Inconsummation

A model for assimilating or healthy sublimating of sexual desires is presented in an intriguing and appealing way by Rolheiser in his book *The Holy Longing*. As noted above, Rolheiser's definition of sexuality has to do with creativity and delight in what is created. He names sexuality as "the greatest energy of all inside us." He further says that sexuality lies at the center of the spiritual life and that "one of the fundamental tasks of spirituality . . . is to help us to understand and channel our sexuality correctly."[75] Rolheiser presents guidelines for what he calls "living in inconsummation" according to Christian perspectives. He compares sexual inconsummation, or incompleteness, to the frustration of a "lifelong unfinished symphony" and suggests what one can do until the Messiah returns to finish the symphony:

1. Understand the time we are living in (the now but not yet).
2. Understand how wide is sexuality's hunger.
3. Turn our inconsummation into solitude.
4. Understand sexual incompleteness as solidarity with the poor.
5. Accept the inadequacy of our love so that its real power can show through.[76]

These profound concepts deserve more study than this book allows, but in essence they put flesh on the concepts of celibacy that guide religious celibates, concepts that seem to be types of holy sublimation.

One of the respondents to the Living Well questionnaire wrote, "Sublimation can be sublime—NOT!" Perhaps inspiration or a sense of the transcendent can occur as one is sublimating sexual energy, but probably not without introspection and intentional effort. We may come to know that we don't have the complete symphony *and* we don't need it all. In some sense, none of us will have the whole symphony on this side of heaven.

Integration of Sexuality, Heart, Head, and Spirituality

I propose a model for living well as a single, sexual, and celibate person that involves both heart and head work, one that integrates sexuality and spirituality. It begins with recognizing erotic feelings, sexual longings, and sexual energy anywhere and everywhere throughout one's body, but often centered in the pelvis. After one has recognized the feelings, one can figuratively—almost literally—draw the feelings up into one's heart. There the energy can be transformed from a desire to draw another person into oneself, from a yearning to almost possess the other, to copious feelings of unselfish love, tenderness, and compassion—feelings that usually "come from the heart."

Along with the heart work, one can also draw the energy into one's head and reflect on its meaning as described above by Joyce. In addition, this can become spiritual work as one reflects on the energy that is part of the longing to know and to be known and reflects on the similarities between the longing for union with God and the longing for union with another person. Thus this work becomes an integration of one's sexuality, both the physical and emotional aspects; one's emotions, particularly aspects of love; one's intellect; and one's spirit as it intersects with and relates to God's Spirit. This integrative model may also include reflection about living with inconsummation.

Celibacy as the Basis for Sex

Gabrielle Brown outlines a secular model for celibacy in the book *The New Celibacy: Why More Men and Women are Abstaining from Sex—and Enjoying it More.* Brown makes a statement that parallels what many of the Catholic celibate theologians say: "Just as silence is the basis for sound, for speech, for music, celibacy it the basis for sex."[77] Although much of the book focuses on periods of celibacy within marriage,[78] Brown also describes single women who practice celibacy and report "good feelings about finally taking charge of their own bodies, . . . experiences of increased energy in all aspects of their lives, . . . feelings of peacefulness, settledness, centeredness, and the development and grow of spiritual life."[79] The striking similarities of the outcomes of celibacy for religious and secular purposes are noteworthy.

We will move from models for celibate living to masturbation. Although masturbation is not a model for celibate living, it is an act that assists many people in dealing with sexual energy during periods when they are celibate.

Masturbation[80]

Throughout much of Christian history, the purpose of sexual intercourse was thought to be procreation only. Augustine's idea that sexual intercourse for the purpose of satisfying sexual desire was sinful, which means of course that masturbation was considered sinful. In addition, masturbation was thought to be unnatural.

In the sexually permissive culture of North America, where sex is openly talked about and billboards and TV ads unabashedly promote sexual products, this aspect of sexuality is still "in the closet" for many people. Masturbation, also called autoeroticism or self-pleasuring, is surrounded by controversy and guilt and is a difficult subject for many people to discuss, due at least in part to the negative attitudes society has traditionally held. Keeping in mind that the Bible says nothing about masturbation,[81] we look to Christian and social history to gain some understandings of views of sexuality throughout the Christian era.

An illustration of the discomfort that even modern, educated people feel in talking about masturbation is given by Stephen Greenblatt who, as chair of a Harvard History and Literature program, invited Thomas Laqueur, author of *Solitary Sex: A Cultural History of Masturbation*, to be a guest lecturer in 2003. The book and Laqueur's lecture enlivened that semester at Harvard, but Greenblatt describes the panic that set in among the instructors who were responsible to lead the seminars following the lecture. He concluded that "masturbation is virtually unique, in the array of more or less universal behaviors, in arousing a peculiar and peculiarly intense current of anxiety."[82]

In his detailed cultural history of masturbation, Laqueur notes that masturbation was first classified as a disease in 1712 when an anonymous author in London published a small tract, *Onania*, about cures for the previously incurable disease. The effects of the tract were apparently far reaching.[83]

Swiss physician Tissot published *L'Onanisme: Ou Dissertation physique sur les maladies produites par la masturbation* in 1770, which also had a significant effect on culture.[84] Laqueur thinks that "masturbation became ethically central and construed as dangerous precisely when its component parts came to be valued," that is, the exploration of individual imagination as part of the Enlightenment.[85] The writing of novels began in this era, and Laqueur suggests that the reading of novels led to the compulsion to link terrible health maladies to masturbation. He shows that reading and masturbation were closely linked to some of the moral criticism of that time, which argued that reading novels and masturbation reinforced each other.[86]

During the next century in North America, Sylvester Graham and J. H. Kellogg invented graham crackers and cornflakes as "anti-masturbation foods." They both wrote best-selling books detailing the terrible ills that befell masturbators. Kellogg informed parents in 1888 that there were no fewer than thirty-nine signs of masturbation. These included acne, bashfulness, boldness, nail biting, use of tobacco, and bedwetting. For prevention he prescribed a healthy lifestyle that included vigorous exercise, sleeping on a hard wooden bed, and a diet that deemphasized meat and highlighted grains—particularly cornflakes, of course.[87]

In *Liberating Sex: A Christian Sexual Theology*, Adrian Thatcher says that it is the "androcentric and anti-body consciousness for which masturbation remains a grave sin."

> Masturbation, the sexual arousal of oneself or another by manual stimulation of the genitals, is a positive, pleasurable activity which only a patriarchal under-

standing of sexuality condemns. . . . In a patriarchal order, the thought that women can obtain sexual pleasure without the presence or permission of men signals a threatening independence. . . . Masturbation, especially for men and women with no other sexual outlet, is a positive force in one's life. Yet most religious writing about masturbation condemns it.[88]

In addition, Thatcher gives the official position of the Catholic Church:

The Vatican's Declaration on Sexual Ethics (1975) reaffirms that masturbation is "gravely sinful" and "an intrinsically and gravely disordered action." This is because "the deliberate use of the sexual faculty, for whatever reason, outside of marriage is essentially contrary to its purpose," and "all deliberate sexual activity must be referred to the married state."[89]

On the other hand, in 1970 the Presbyterian General Assembly of the United Presbyterian Church produced a statement published in the booklet *Sexuality and the Human Community*. The final paragraph states,

Since masturbation is often one of the earliest pleasurable sexual experiences which is identifiably genital, we consider it essential that the church, through its teachings and through the attitudes it encourages in Christian homes, contribute to a healthy understanding of this experience which will be free of guilt and shame. The ethical significance of masturbation depends entirely on the context in which it takes place. Therefore, we can see no objection to it when it occurs as a normal developmental experience or as a deliberately chosen alternative to inappropriate heterosexual activity. We can see valid ethical questions raised about masturbatory practices which . . . inhibit normal heterosexual development. In most instances, however, we believe that masturbation is morally neutral and psychologically benign.[90]

In a 1989 Presbyterian program for teaching sexuality in the church, four paragraphs on masturbation are included. The final paragraph is,

What does our church believe about masturbation? Masturbation is a normal part of growing up. There should be no guilt or shame for engaging in masturbation. Although we believe our sexuality is to be shared with someone else, masturbation can be a good choice to make in some circumstances.[91]

There has been little published by Mennonite presses on masturbation. In 1972 *With* magazine (for youth in the Mennonite Church) published an article entitled "What about Masturbation" by an anonymous author.[92] The responses that followed the publication of that article included numerous comments about guilt and shame that had up until then plagued the responders. J. Lorne Peachey, who edited *With* when the masturbation article appeared, has written *What Really Matters: Conversation Starters for Men* along with Everett Thomas. The issue of masturbation is addressed in a few paragraphs in a chapter entitled "Sex." Peachey and Thomas refer to masturbation as "likely the most common but least talked about issue related to sex." They suggest that each person must make a decision about masturbation, making that decision in prayer and honest conversation with a spiritual companion.[93]

My search for other Mennonite publications with references to masturbation produced only two items between 1972 and 2002. One is a reference in *The Mennonite Mosaic: Identity and Modernization* by J. Howard Kauffman and Leo Driedger. They reported on their studies within the Mennonite Church, which indicated an increasing acceptance of masturbation. In 1972, 46 percent of respondents said that masturbation is "always wrong," whereas in 1989, 34 percent responded that it is "always wrong."[94]

Human Sexuality in the Christian Life: A Working Document for Study and Dialogue, which includes responses from the Mennonite Church and the General Conference Mennonite Church, was published in 1985. The section on masturbation includes the following:

> Although the Bible does not speak about masturbation, the popular assumption promoted by both church and society is that it is harmful to the person. Words which

do not evoke the same negative feeling are self-stimulation, auto-eroticism or solo-sex. (The word, masturbation, comes from two Latin words: manus [hand] and turbatio [agitation or excitement].)

One has to distinguish the motive for masturbation, its frequency, and the situation of the person if one is going to understand the meaning of masturbatory activity. Reasons for self-stimulation are many. An adolescent might masturbate out of curiosity. A married individual separated from his/her spouse might masturbate because he/she is accustomed to genital relations.

Exploration before puberty is simply a part of normal growth. Adolescent masturbation often comes with puberty. . . . The majority masturbate during this period. An adolescent boy can be absorbed with the mystery of an erection and spontaneously experiment in order to discover its meaning. At this time, masturbation can easily become a habit.

While most discussion centers around the masturbation of puberty, nevertheless, there is also adult masturbation, an activity which might not be pursued if other options were available. Examples of adult masturbation include: university students who have chosen not to marry might masturbate in order to avoid unwanted premarital intercourse; a widow or widower who finds herself or himself without the same genital life as before. The issue here is one of genital and physiological tension which might need release especially if the person were accustomed to physical relations prior to separation.

For many single adults, occasional masturbation is an outlet for tension. Adult masturbation differs from adolescent masturbation in that the adult person should have integrated his or her sexuality into his or her life more than the adolescent has, and the adult would express his or her genitality with someone he or she loves rather than alone if that were possible.

Does masturbation lead to better emotional health? How does it relate to the total well being of the person? Psychological problems caused by masturbation do not arise from the masturbatory activity but from the individual's and society's attitude toward it. If a person's feelings about sexuality are clouded with guilt, fear, and confusion, the results for that individual could be harmful. Masturbation to avoid interpersonal relationships can be a sign of inner distress. Within a marriage, if masturbation is used as the exclusive sexual release when sexual relations are possible, it may signal a lack of wholesome relationship or a deeper problem within the individual.

The fundamental question is, how does our sexual practice serve our relationship to God and our relationship to others? In the light of this, the significance of masturbation diminishes.[95]

Looking beyond Mennonite circles, a theological and ethical analysis of masturbation is found in a chapter entitled "The Place of Pleasure" in *Wisdom of the Body: Making Sense of Our Sexuality* by Whitehead and Whitehead.[96] In the field of sexuality today there is almost unanimous agreement that "autoeroticism is healthy, desirable, and important to adult sexual adjustment."[97] For many it serves as a reliever of sexual tension. Some have proposed that it is a gift or a grace.

Masturbation may lend a helpful hand to a person who lacks genital intimacy, and for widowed or single people it may be the best option for relieving sexual tension. However, it may be that as a person develops various kinds of nongenital but intimate relationships, the desire to masturbate may decrease. One might ask, "Can masturbation lead one to the temple?" (using the image that Rohr uses to describe a good sexual experience). Perhaps it can. The experience of openness, of total giving and total receiving, of knowing and being known that accompanies the physiological ecstasy of orgasm can be a spiritual encounter.

When a relationship that had many layers of intimacy ends suddenly, as in the death of a spouse, a person can be very intimacy-deprived, especially if he or she does not have many other intimate friendships. It can take a great deal of time for friendships to develop significant levels of emotional and social intimacy. In the meantime, while one may not have the energy to invest in new or deeper friendships, masturbation can be a way to experience intimacy with the self or a fantasized person.

Masturbation is a concern for many widowed people. Some people experience diminishment or loss of sexual drive for a time following the death of a spouse, but sexual longings usually return eventually. A number of the popular books for widowed people have information about sexuality. About half of the secular books refer to sexuality, but most of them make the assumption that widowed people will become sexually involved with another person. The only question seems to be how soon after the death a new sexual liaison is appropriate. Most Christian books for widowed people do not deal directly with sexuality, and the majority of those that do are rather vague.

In a three-year period of reading and surveying dozens of books for widowed people, I found only two that deal with masturbation. One is *Getting to the Other Side of Grief: Overcoming the Loss of a Spouse*. The authors of this book write from a Christian perspective and state very matter-of-factly that self-pleasuring or masturbation "is an option available to single persons to help reduce the physiological sexual tension that develops as part of being human."[98] They hardly allow masturbating simply for pleasure—as the term self-pleasuring suggests.

Another reference is in *Widowed* by Joyce Brothers. She encourages women to masturbate so as not to "feel like a needy sexually-deprived person."[99]

Findings of the Living Well Study

I used the opportunity of my study to ask questions about masturbation. My sampling of people who had been celibate[100] for a time after presumably being sexually active[101] at an earlier time was a good population of which to ask such questions. In designing the questionnaire, I made the assumption that most widowed people practice celibacy for at least a period of time, regardless of whether they eventually enter into other sexual relationships. On the basis of this assumption I asked three questions about celibate sexuality.

To try to determine the range of what is "normal" regarding sexual interest after spousal death, the following was asked: "Adults have varying degrees of sexual longings that may or may not change after being widowed. What changes, if any, have you experienced?" Of the 61 percent of the respondents who answered this question, 59 were women and 33 were men. Of those, 16 percent said they did not note any changes in the degree of sexual longings after the spousal death. However, it is likely that some who did not answer the question may also be in this category.

Twenty-one percent said or implied that their sexual longings increased or continued to be intense after spousal death. Only 11 percent said specifically that the degree of sexual longings decreased. Twenty-two percent gave neutral responses to the question about sexual longings, noting the presence of sexual desire but not commenting on whether it increased or decreased. One person wrote, "I would enjoy intimacy but I don't crave sex most of the time." Another responded, "For the first three years it seemed there were so many major crises that these needs did not seem important."

I had heard of the myth that widows are very needy sexually and that too many men, believing or perhaps hoping in the myth, have offered their sexual services to young widows. After being widowed myself, I began to read and hear that men, often married and sometimes friends, were indeed offering themselves sexually to widowed women. I became extremely cautious, determining to wear my wedding ring on my left hand for a long time and not telling men who came to work on my house that I was widowed. A few times I even referred to my husband's preferences as though he were still alive. Fortunately, I managed to avoid any advances from strangers, and all my friends have been trustworthy.

My relatively small sampling indicates that the percentages of women and men with increased or intense sexual longings are nearly the same. One person wrote, "For the first few months I did not think about sex at all. Then it hit me like a tidal wave—great waves of sexual desire." Others said they very much missed the sexual relationship but did not indicate whether desires were greater or less than before.

Shuchter suggests that increased sexual interest following spousal death may be a response to the loss of many layers of intimacy that typically occurs with a spouse's death. Since the height of intimacy occurs in the sexual relationship for many couples, "the newly bereaved person may turn toward sexual relationships to create the illusion that they have again achieved such intimacy and saved themselves from pain."[102]

While this is likely true for some people, feelings of intense longing may occur in part due to the profound sense of emptiness a widowed person experiences after the death. We are created with the need for relationship, the desire to know and be known, and as we've noted, our sexuality and spirituality are closely entwined. Feeling disconnected from God, as some do after the death of a loved one, may bring a tremendous sense of longing to be loved and accepted, to know and be known. There may be some relief of this intense longing when personal barriers melt away as happens at the time of orgasm.

Another group of people who responded to the question about sexual longings in the Living Well study did not answer directly but made varied comments about their sexuality, such as, "I developed the awareness that emotional intimacy is more important than sexual intimacy." Several of these respondents mentioned the impact their loved one's illness had on their sexual relationship.

The second sexuality question was, "If you have been celibate for periods of time, what have you done (or do you do) with your sexual energy?"[103] Of the 105 who responded to this question (69 women, 35 men), 59 percent said they try or had tried to channel sexual energy into wholesome activities. Fifty-five percent said they masturbate(d). This included 45 percent of women who responded to this question and 74 percent of men.[104] In decreasing frequency, respondents said they stayed busy, took the opportunity to learn about themselves, talked about it with close friends, and remained frustrated.

The third question regarding sexuality in the Living Well study was about fantasy. One concern about masturbation is related to the fantasies that accompany masturbation for most people. One study showed that fantasies or daydreams are part of masturbation for about 75 percent of males who masturbate and about half of females. Some authors note that masturbation without fantasy may be unhealthy because it "then becomes purely a mechanical act without any interpersonal sexual overtones."[105] And as Whitehead and Whitehead note, "Sexual arousal is meant to move us toward other people."[106] If a sexual activity does not lead to someone or something beyond oneself, then perhaps it should be questioned.

The question of fantasy in masturbation is one that seems to be little pursued, but is perhaps the question that needs to be addressed when considering whether there may be an element of sin in masturbation.[107]

Foster wrote,

> Masturbation's sexual fantasies are a very real part of human life that needs to be disciplined, not eliminated. Erotic imaginings will come; the real ethical question is how to deal with them. . . . Can they be brought into proper perspective within the far greater matters of love and human relationship? We like fantasies because they idealize life. In our fantasies we are the paradigm of sexual prowess, our partner is desirable beyond compare. . . . This is precisely why fantasies need discipline: they can divorce us from the real world of human imperfection.[108]

Reasons that masturbation is considered unacceptable by some people are listed by Douglas Rosenau. These include fantasies, selfishness, and the possibility that masturbation may lead to wrong sexual activity.

> Most of sexuality is in one's mind—the emotional and physical reactions that the mind has learned to trigger

when various stimuli are present. Fantasy does not equal lust and there is a difference between thinking about something and doing it. In fact, fantasy keeps the relational factor within masturbation.[109]

Ethicist Joseph Kotva wonders about fantasy's power to shape our character and form us morally over time. Social science has shown that visual images have an amazing ability to shape and code the way we see the world. Does something similar happen when we close our eyes in fantasy? Do fantasies shape and form us? "If so," Kotva says, "the content of our fantasies matters a great deal because they move us toward or away from becoming certain kinds of people with certain kinds of propensities."[110]

Regarding sexual fantasy, we need to consider Jesus' words: "You have heard that it was said, 'You shall not commit adultery.' But I say to you that everyone who looks at a woman with lust has already committed adultery with her in his heart" (Matthew 5:27-28). These verses are set in a context of six "antitheses" in which Matthew shows how Jesus revised and deepened the teaching of Old Testament law. In this saying, Jesus is referring to male religious leaders who thought that by refraining from adultery, they were morally and religiously righteous. Thatcher emphasizes that this passage is not a condemnation of fantasy. It is rather a condemnation of religious arrogance.[111]

Joyce Brothers says it is impossible for a widow to think about her deceased spouse while masturbating, "because the thought that he is not with you is too painful [and] pain and sex are incompatible."[112]

The question asked in this study was, "If you masturbate(d), whom do/did you fantasize or think about at that time?" Options were

___ my deceased spouse
___ a nonspecific other person
___ a specific other person
___ other

Of the 31 women and 26 men[113] who indicated that they masturbate or had done so, 43 percent said they fantasized about the deceased spouse; 22 percent fantasized about a specific other person; and 31 percent fantasized about a nonspecific other.

One person, who as Brothers suggested was unable to fantasize about the deceased spouse, added that all fantasies were about single "available" people. While relieved that dealing with adultery in fantasies was not an issue (because in the fantasy neither he nor the fantasized partner were married to someone else), this person was pleasantly surprised that for him such a clear sexual ethic existed at the fantasy level as well as in reality.

While acknowledging that masturbation is indeed a personal and private affair, bringing conversations about the morality of masturbation into the open might help to relieve some of the guilt and shame long associated with this behavior. The benefits of such discussions include recognizing it as a natural tendency and a phase through which many people go as they move toward interpersonal relationships. In addition, removing the feelings of guilt may free people to seek psychological and spiritual help to deal with fantasies that are abusive or degrading to self or others.

When feelings of guilt or shame are removed, masturbation may be understood as a gift. It can be an opportunity to enjoy the beauty and mystery of sexuality, this greatest of energies that God created in humanity. Thanking God for the gift of sexuality as experienced in an autoerotic act will offer one peace of mind and a greater understanding of oneself as created in the image of God.[114]

To conclude this section on masturbation, I refer to a story told by Rolheiser about a professor who was in the middle of a lecture in a graduate class on sexuality and morality when he was asked if he masturbates. Although first thinking the question was out of order, the professor decided to answer, saying, "Yes, sometimes I do—and I'm not proud of it. I don't think it's very wrong and I don't think it's very right either." However, he was sure that he was a better person when he did not masturbate, "because then I am carrying more of the tension that we, all of us, should carry in this life. I'm a better person when I carry that tension."[115]

Rather than placing a moral judgment on masturbation or sexual attractions or dating relationships, this study points to the conclusion that all of these experiences are opportunities for reflection, new and deeper understandings of oneself, and occasions for growth. Paying attention to one's inner life is accepting the invitation to transformation and leads to living well following the death of a spouse.

Part 3

Looking
Forward

Implications for Pastoral Care

I said to the person at the gate of the year:
"Give me a light that I may tread safely into the unknown."
That person said to me:
"Go out into the darkness and
place your hand into the hand of God.
That will be to you better than a light
and safer than a known way."
—Minnie Louise Haskins[1]

We will now turn our attention to friendship and pastoral care that we hope will be available to all who struggle on journeys of grief after losing a husband or wife in death. This final chapter includes suggestions I have gathered from AMBS classroom lectures and sermons, from a variety of written resources, from responses to the Living Well study, from my observations, and from my experience as a widow, a pastoral person, and a friend.

The Living Well study produced an abundance of data about how pastoral care and friendship were experienced by widowed people. Many of the observations and remarks of respondents have direct implications for pastoral care.

Of course, providing pastoral care is not limited to ministers employed by churches. Offering pastoral care is for all who follow Jesus. Following Jesus includes belonging to a community of faith, which of itself is a means of extending pastoral care, and indeed the body of Christ is needed to support those who offer pastoral care.

If the pastoral-care needs of all the wounded people in our communities are to be met, more people will need to accept this calling. Time and time again we hear that the *words* spoken by people at the time of the death of a loved one are not nearly as important as the *presence* of caring people. Anyone can offer presence, and silent attendance is sometimes the most profound kind of presence, because words are often woefully inadequate.

It is helpful for caregivers to have grappled with questions of life and death and to have an understanding of human development and spiritual growth as well as some knowledge of loss, grief, and mourning. Profound, insightful, and effective care of hurting people often comes from people who are "wounded healers." At the same time, people who have not suffered great losses can also learn to be compassionate and supportive.

It is important for pastors and friends of the bereaved to be aware that mourning the death of a loved one is work that goes on and on. The face of grief changes and the intensity diminishes over time, but for most people the loss will demand attention for a long time. For grieving people to continue on journeys of hope with a sense of joy and peace, it will be helpful if they and their caregivers attend to issues addressed in this chapter.

Considerations for Pastoral Care of Bereaved People

With compassion and infinite love, God cares for all creation. Caring for the bereaved and suffering is God's work. Those who offer friendship and pastoral care to the suffering and bereaved join God in the work of healing and reconciliation that God is already doing in the world. The ministry of Jesus is the ultimate model for offering pastoral care, though there are other models useful for caregivers as they attempt to follow Jesus in caring for others.

Spiritual Direction

The model of spiritual director or spiritual guide is one that can inform a caregiver when relating to bereaved people. Because each person is unique, each loss has its distinct characteristics, and because there are many ways to mourn a loss, an approach that does not promote specific answers is desirable. The focus of spiritual direction as it has been practiced by Christians for centuries is on the relationship of the directee (or seeker) and God. The director or guide does not come to the directee with answers and directions, but prayerfully—with a commitment to listen, with attention to God's movement in the directee's life, and with openness to the Holy Spirit's direction. In addition to telling her or his story and asking questions, the seeker's task is to pay attention to God, to listen, and to work on issues that arise.

The spiritual direction model operates with the recognition that God's Spirit is at work with all humanity and that those who pay attention to the activity of God's Spirit interacting with the human spirit will find answers to life's questions and discover ways to respond to issues. Formal spiritual direction is an excellent way for any person who is dealing with tough questions to address those issues, especially those that emerge during bereavement. However, the principles of spiritual direction can be utilized by any listener who wants to walk with a struggling friend.

The role of a friend, pastor, or spiritual director is not to try to direct the healing process, but rather to remove obstacles that may impede mourning and spiritual growth. A listening ear may be the most important gift a friend or caregiver can offer a bereaved person. Telling the story of the loss is something that most people need to do repeatedly. We tell our stories to confirm the reality of the loss and to try to make sense of life. When we tell them, we remove some of grief's power over us and "become empowered to reconstruct our present reality" in a way that accounts for the loss and lays to rest some of the past, "without obliterating the continued healing presence of memory."[2] As a bereaved person repeats the story to an attentive listener, new insights may come to light, insights that help him or her move along on the journey. But people should share their stories of pain and loss only when they are ready and in a place where there is great caring, safety, and trust. Attempting to create such a place is part of pastoral care work.

Crucial to providing spiritual direction is that the guide has an active, healthy, and growing relationship with God for which he or she is accountable to another Christian or group of Christians. Practicing spiritual disciplines assists one in listening to God, in listening to the other, and in listening to God in the other.

Narrative Pastoral Counseling

Another model for pastoral care is the narrative approach designed by Christie Cozad Nueger and described in her book *Counseling Women: A Narrative, Pastoral Approach*. The practices for pastoral counseling she describes are especially applicable to pastoral care of bereaved people. Her "liberating and effective" practices are a commitment to empowerment, justice, grace, and interdependency.[3] Neuger's model is presented as applying specifically to women and not necessarily concerning loss issues, but the applications to pastoral care of bereaved men and women are striking. The four-fold approach to counseling that she presents is helping people come to voice (that is, discovering a way to express a heretofore unexpressed idea, feeling or experience), gain clarity about their stories, make choices that are helpful, moral, and hopeful, and stay connected in relationships and community. These are also pertinent goals for pastoral care for bereaved people.

In addition, Neuger utilizes narrative counseling theory,

which has parallels in spiritual direction. Narrative counseling theory is respectful and efficient, using a consultative model rather than an expert model. The main focus is not on the relationship between counselor and counselee but on those between the counselee and others. The theory is "based on hope and on the foundational reality that human beings are makers of meaning at their deepest core and that reality is constructed as we make meaning out of our experience."[4] The process becomes therapeutic as "problem narratives" are identified and deconstructed, the problem is externalized, and healthy self-narratives are reconstructed.[5]

Neuger identifies five activities for gaining clarity: remembering, reframing, reversing, re-imagining and re-storying.[6] These are similar to the four aspects of "praying our goodbye" as described by Joyce Rupp: recognition, reflection, ritualization, and reorientation.[7] In fact, walking with a bereaved person as she or he faces the "tasks of mourning" as described in chapter 2 could also be thought of as a patterned process for providing pastoral care.

"The Way of Wisdom"[8]

Wisdom in the light of God is the ground metaphor that Daniel Schipani uses in his book on pastoral counseling. This wisdom is an integration of psychological and theological perspectives and sees the pastoral counselor as ethicist and moral guide.[9] Schipani calls all pastors serving congregations to be "caregiving sages," counseling people who confront the challenges and struggles of life. This work is to be done, "not as mental health professionals in the psychiatric sense, but as ministers of the gospel and worthy representatives of the caring, healing Christ."[10]

When pastoral counseling is understood to be the "practice of wisdom, [then] . . . the goal . . . [for the counselee is] growth in wisdom—knowing how to live well—in the light of God." This concept re-envisions pastoral counseling as follows:

- It must be viewed, practiced, and taught pastorally.
- It must be contextualized ecclesiologically.
- It must be centered on Jesus Christ as the Wisdom of God.
- It must be grounded in Scripture.
- It must be viewed, practiced and taught as a unique form of the (re)creative process guided by the Spirit.
- It must be oriented toward the reign of God.[11]

Being a "Wounded Healer"

All humanity suffers loss and pain. Some of the "gifts of grief" identified by respondents to the Living Well questionnaire included becoming more compassionate, understanding, and loving. Many individuals emerge from a time of loss or suffering with renewed vigor and vision, and are called to offer ministries like those from which they have benefited. In this way, many become "wounded healers." Henri Nouwen made this concept familiar in his book, *The Wounded Healer.* He broadened the idea, saying that ministers are called to recognize their own suffering and make that very recognition the starting point of service to others. [12]

However, being a wounded healer is not just repeating for another wounded person what we have found helpful in our woundedness, but it is being formed and transformed by the suffering of Jesus and the suffering in the world around us in addition to our personal suffering. Nouwen wrote,

> On the one hand, no minister can keep his own experience of life hidden from those he wants to help. Nor should he want to keep it hidden. While a doctor can still be a good doctor even when his private life is severely disrupted, no minister can offer service without a constant and vital acknowledgment of his own experiences. On the other hand, it would be very easy to misuse the concept of the wounded healer by defending a form of spiritual exhibitionism. A minister who talks in the pulpit about his own personal problems is of no help to his

congregation, for no suffering human being is helped by someone who tells him that he has the same problems. . . . Making one's own wounds a source of healing, therefore, does not call for a sharing of superficial personal pains but for a constant willingness to see one's own pain and suffering as rising from the depth of the human condition which all [people] share.[13]

Many caregivers offer extremely effective care because of their depths of understanding of what it is to be wounded. On the other hand, attempting to minister out of one's own pain that has not come to some level of resolution can lead to ineffective ministry and can even be dangerous. The "client" who expects to receive something from the "healer" may end up offering care to the one who was supposedly the healer. A caregiver should not discuss with a "client" a personal problem with which he or she is currently struggling. Only if the caregiver has come to a satisfactory working resolution of the problem is it appropriate to talk about it with the one to whom care is being offered.

In her stimulating book *Resurrection Psychology*, Margaret Alter exposes deep truths in the chapter "Significance of Scars." She claims that "it is our scars that make us credible, and it is our scars that make us sensitive."[14] During the years that I worked as an obstetrical nurse, a point that was never totally resolved for me was whether a woman who had never given birth could be an outstanding obstetrical nurse. A good nurse, yes. An effective nurse, of course. But an outstanding obstetrical nurse, maybe not. So shall we trust a person who does not limp, who does not have scars, who has not been wounded? Consider that to walk with a dying person we cannot have experienced physical death. Indeed, this is one of the places in which Christian ministry is superior to all others. We have within us the Spirit of Jesus who suffered and died, and it is that Spirit within us that makes us credible more than anything else.

When we reflect on the above models, we recognize

numerous practices that were used by Jesus in his ministry: paying attention to the recipient's relationship with God, asking prompting questions, and listening as is done in spiritual direction; the use of story as in the narrative approach; practicing wisdom in the light of God; and living as a wounded healer.

Providing care for others is holy work to which all Christians are called. Jesus said that when we serve "the least of these" we are helping to bring about the reign of God. Many people offer care to others as situations arise in day-to-day living. For others, caregiving is a vocation to which they have been especially called. For the latter there are special considerations.

Self-Care for Caregivers

There are many resources that emphasize the importance of caregivers taking care of themselves in order to remain effective and avoid burnout or compassion fatigue. In an essay entitled "If I Am Not for Myself: Caring for Yourself as a Caregiver for Those Who Grieve," James E. Miller begins with the following questions from Rabbi Hillel:

If I am not for myself, who will be for me?
But if I am only for myself, what am I?
And if not now, when?[15]

Miller's guidelines include the following:

• Accept the fact you cannot do this work alone and still do it well.
• Understand you cannot do this work without letup.
• Practice what you preach: wholeness.
• Model what you stand for: healing and growth.
• In the midst of heaviness, you can always find ways to be light.
• Befriend your helplessness.
• Practice letting go.
• Treat your work for what it is: a calling.[16]

It is absolutely essential for caregivers to practice self-care. They should recognize their own limits and vulnerabilities, and attend to the warning signs of fatigue and burnout. Taking weekly Sabbath time is necessary for one to be nurtured and sustained.

Practitioners need to attend to their own wounds, and when they experience loss and grief, they need to mourn just like anyone else. Having some understanding of grief does not mean they do not need to do it. It may mean that they know a little better how to proceed. Caregivers can be present to another's grief only to the extent that they have recognized and attended to their own grief.

Pastoral caregivers must intentionally attend to their own spiritual needs. This can be done through formal spiritual direction or spiritual friendship. In addition, a plan should be in place for professional consultation when additional wisdom is needed for complicated situations.

Ongoing Agenda for Pastoral Caregivers

To offer effective pastoral care to grieving people, caregivers must attend to their own questions about life and death and must have some basic understandings about loss, grief, and mourning. It is also helpful to understand the value of rituals for difficult transitions. Forming a thoughtful, well-grounded theology of death will help to prepare one for responding to death crises.

Reflect Theologically on Living and Dying

Foundational for Christians offering care to bereaved people is having beliefs about life and death that are accountable to the major themes of the Bible. The fact that bereaved people come face to face with life and death questions was addressed in chapter 3. In this section the emphasis is on the caregiver grappling with her or his own issues surrounding terminal illness, dying, death, and bereavement.

Nouwen emphasized the importance of ministers being contemplative, always looking for signs of hope and promise. A ministering person must be able to articulate the inner events of life, because only those who are able to

articulate their own experiences can be a "source of clari-
fication" for others.[17] In addition, it is important that caregivers understand the value of rituals and practices that
immediately follow death in order to accompany a person
through subsequent months and years.

David Tripp contends that one can address the meaning
of death only when one looks at the liturgy of death. It
behooves pastors to study the liturgy of death and be prepared to lead bereaved people through a liturgy that will
help to prepare them for the days, months, and years following the time when the community enacts the liturgy.
The liturgy is not about what the people do; it is about
what God is doing. We join in the work that God has
already begun.[18]

The editorial and numerous essays in the Spring 2004
issue of *Vision: A Journal for Church and Theology* are
excellent resources for dealing with death issues. In her
essay "After a Death: Theology and Christian Funeral
Practices," Gayle Gerber Koontz identifies classic Christian
themes that serve as points from which foundational affirmations can be made, affirmations that can help us review
Christian practices surrounding death. These are fundamental to offering effective pastoral care at the time of a
death and following. Key points include the following:

1. Especially within the church, death is a community event, not an individual or private family
   matter.

2. Christian funeral services are worship services
   and should focus on God, not on the one who
   has died. Death is part of the cycle of "genesis,
   change, growth, decay, and death" established
   by Creator God as the plan for living things.

3. Because "humans are whole beings in whom
   body and spirit are indissolubly linked" and
   because people are God's in death as well as in
   life, human bodies are to be treated with respect
   before and after death.

4. "Jesus is both example and revelation" as we deal with issues related to death.

5. There are numerous ways in which, at the time of a death, pastors and others can give expression to God's love and grace, faithfulness, mercy, and hope.[19]

Pastoral care providers will be helped in their tasks by pondering the above. In addition, education of people within congregations is extremely important, especially in these days of individualism. Cases of not having a time of public mourning are occurring even within the church. Alan Wolfelt predicts that our culture is fast moving in the direction of "drive-through funerals," where visitors can view a photo of the deceased and register their names.[20] Already one can register on the Internet an acknowledgment of having read an obituary. This seems to follow the pattern of death-avoidance and death-denial that has been growing in North America in recent decades. As Christians we have an opportunity to promote the biblical counter-cultural response to death.

Minister in Light of the Death and Resurrection of Jesus

Living in light of the death and resurrection of Jesus is entering into mystery and embracing paradox. Jesus uses paradox in his sayings about the kingdom of God and in his parabolic teaching: the outcomes of the parables are unexpected and unconventional. Alter points out that the parables of Jesus are a "continual warning about the danger of certainty: constant disruption of what is presumed deserved, earned, and controlled." Jesus' stories and his life offer an ongoing invitation to live within our finitude (the limitations of our finiteness), while at the same time experiencing love and empowerment from God.[21]

To provide effective pastoral care, one should consider Alter's question "What is our identity of caring that empowers but does not rescue, is wholehearted but not certain?" Compassionate concern for others is the central message of the law and the prophets upon which Jesus builds. Integral to his teachings is concern for others. Yes, "we are called to a vocation of concern, but only within the confines of finitude."[22] In this work of caring for others we experience powerlessness, pain, and misery. We can never do enough.

We may feel like giving up. But then we look at the Beatitudes, and we see the paradox. Alter writes, "As a species and as a culture we put maximum effort into denial of death, denial of suffering, denial of powerlessness . . . denial of our finitude." But Jesus turns things around. In the Beatitudes he invites us to mourn for the suffering in the world and fully embrace "our sense of finite powerlessness." In so doing, we come to recognize "that the blessing is in the grieving, [the] blessing is in the finitude." Furthermore, "a vocation of concern set in the powerlessness of our finitude [enhances] our lived perception of abundant life and mental health." This attitude assists both bereaved and caregiver, for "when we accept Jesus' challenge to a vocation of concern in the midst of our finitude, we make a choice for greater experience of empathic suffering, but also richer health and deeper joy."[23]

Study Loss, Grief, and Mourning

Loss and grief are such complex subjects that even those who make decades-long serious studies of them do not master them. Although most pastors will not have the opportunity to become certified grief counselors, it is important that they be knowledgeable about loss, grief, and mourning. Unresolved loss and grief issues can cause difficulties for people indefinitely. A friend who works in a mental health facility estimates that 75 percent of her clients have unresolved loss issues at the root of the problems for which they seek treatment.

Guidelines for those who care for people who grieve the death of loved ones include not putting any limits on grief. A group of people who had been widowed between four and ten years were asked for their thoughts about a length of time for healing after spousal death. One said he hates the word *closure*, as he was sure he would never experience closure on the termination of his marriage. Another said, "I don't think one ever recovers from the death of a spouse, but adjustment is necessary." A man who was depressed reported that after five years "grief remains a major theme [but] if I could be blessed again by gaining a person for me to love and be loved by, I think my grief could finally be resolved." It seems that this man was hoping for too much from a relationship with a woman.

One woman whose husband had died more than nine years earlier responded,

> I guess it would be true that daily, I still think of him—especially [when going to] the empty bed—[the place where] we shared our day and talked over our problems and plans for the next day. I wish I could call him—so maybe, I am not to that point yet [where grief is no longer the dominant theme of my life].

Recognizing the wide range of normal emotional responses to the death of a loved one is important. Fortunately, there seems to be no end to resources about loss, grief, and mourning. An annotated bibliography of books particularly suited to widowed people is included in the back of this book. But what is helpful for one person may not be helpful for the next.

One widower found he couldn't read about grief or journal his feelings. Although he was normally a reader and a writer, during his early months of widowhood he could do neither. Instead he moved through his grief by driving, biking, and walking, often in silence. Motion seemed to become a ritual for him.

Many bereaved people experience mystical connections with their deceased loved ones, for example in dreams and intuition. This can be startling for someone who has never paid attention to the realm of the spiritual world. The concept of after-death "communication" is a subject that scientists have recently begun to seriously explore. Edie

Devers, one of the field's preeminent researchers, takes this "extraordinary yet misunderstood phenomenon out of the shadows and brings it into the light" in her book *Goodbye Again.*[24]

The idea of after-death "communication" has some psychological and theological problems that may be difficult to reconcile.[25] For Christians the phenomenon of the communion of the saints may dovetail with experiences of after-death communication. The fascinating and well-studied subject of dreams also has parallels to communion of the saints and after-death communication. It should be noted that dreams about and perceived communication with the deceased often begin many months or even years after the death. These are areas that caregivers should be familiar with, respect, and be open to talking about with people who grieve.

Finally, the study of loss, grief, and mourning should be informed by human development perspectives. Having some theoretical understanding of human growth and spiritual development is foundational to being an effective pastoral caregiver. Theoretical and practical resources that assist caregivers in their ministry to people throughout the life cycle are readily available. Further, learning about personality and psychological assessment, the Enneagram, and the Myers-Briggs Type Indicator can also enhance a caregiver's assistance to a bereaved person.

Assist with Expressions of Pain and Anger

As was noted in chapter 2, biblical lament is a model for mourning. Lament often includes expression of pain or anger. There is a purpose in the feelings of pain and anger. For example, physical pain caused by a splinter in a finger calls attention to the problem. The message is, Remove this foreign body or an infection will occur. Emotional pain invites or demands (depending on the severity) one to pay attention. So it is with anger: the message is that change is required. When anger exists, a pastoral care goal would be to help the individual recognize it and find ways to address it so that its expression can result in self-healing.[26] Anger at God must be expressed in order for one to maintain a relationship with God. Not to express one's feelings is ultimately destructive to a relationship.

This work of enabling bereaved individuals or groups to lament is important work for ministers in roles such as preacher, pastoral care visitor, and spiritual director. It is usually, perhaps always, necessary for laments to be expressed before healing can begin.

There are many good resources for helping people lament the death of loved ones, pray psalms of lament from the Bible, or write their own psalms of lament, including *Psalms of Lament* by Anne Weems, *Rachel's Cry: Prayer of Lament and Rebirth of Hope* by Billman and Migliore, and the chapter "Lamentations: The Pastoral Work of Pain-Sharing" in *Five Smooth Stones for Pastoral Work* by Eugene Peterson.

Lead in Liturgical Lament

The discussion of lament in chapter 2 focused on the perspective of an individual who suffers or mourns. There is also an important component to lament that involves community. Peterson writes that the biblical style of lament is communal, noting that when people in the biblical narrative wept, they wept within community. Therefore, "one of the strategies of pastoral work is to enter private grief and make [it] a shared event. . . . The biblical way to deal with suffering is to transform what is individual into something corporate."[27] A congregation's laments can help to build a bridge to God for suffering people who cannot find the words to speak for themselves. Ron Guengerich recommends that those who are not personally lamenting join the congregation's cries and put into first person the prayers of those who are lamenting.[28] Peterson notes what occurs when "private grief is integrated into communal lament":

1. The act of suffering develops significance . . . there is "consensual validation" that the suffering means something.
2. Community participation insures a human environment . . . [giving the community an expansion of] its distinctiveness as a human community as over against the mob.
3. Sanction is given for the expression of the loss—the outpouring of emotion is legitimized in such a way as to provide catharsis and then renewal.[29]

He clarifies further:

> Pastoral work among the suffering wears a path between home and sanctuary—listens to the poured out, individualized grief and brings it into the sanctuary where it becomes part of the common grief, is placed at the foot of the cross and subjected to the powers of salvation that are diagrammed in all theologies of the atonement.[30]

Thus, the work of pastors includes being aware of people whose grief may need to be "brought to the sanctuary" beyond the days of the funeral and an annual All Saints' Day or Eternity Sunday service. This may include naming bereaved people in pastoral prayers and helping those struggling with grief to find meaningful rituals to express their grief. On certain occasions the role of the minister is to lead individuals or congregations in crying out to God, perhaps using words from the psalms such as "My God, my God, why have you forsaken me? Why are you so far from helping me, from the words of my groaning?" (Psalm 22:1). John Rempel states,

> To enable a congregation to bring such deep distress to God is a profound priestly/pastoral function. Through such expression, the congregation can acknowledge things as they are and begin to rekindle its hope in God, so that God's healing can flow even in the midst of impossible, immobilizing, totally unacceptable situations, leading us to give thanks for God's goodness.[31]

It was noted in chapter 2 that many bereaved people have difficulty going to church and that this might be related to the fact that our corporate worship often does not leave a space for lament. It is important to remember that "no act of worship can proceed without a concern for the condition of those who suffer or who are oppressed," according to J. David Pleins, who also says, "Authentic worship emerges when worshipers dare to express their pain and raise before God their deepest questions." Furthermore, "for the psalmist, the question of participation in worship automatically raises the issue of justice. . . . We are not forced to choose between an internal spirituality and external acts of liberation. The two go hand in hand."[32] When one member or part of a community suffers, the community must allow itself to also feel the suffering and express its pain.

In *Ritual and Pastoral Care*, Elaine Ramshaw says, "It is important to remember that liturgy etymologically means the work of the people, not the work of the pastor. The pastor's work is to midwife the labor of the people of God. . . . Ritual is a way to establish order, to reaffirm meaning, to bond community, to handle ambivalence, and to encounter mystery."[33]

North American Christian rituals and liturgy typically serve bereaved people well in the immediate days following a death. What is lacking in so many cases are rituals and liturgy to help sustain a bereaved person after the initial crisis. Some traditions and individual congregations commemorate All Saints' Day in the fall of the year, but most Christian traditions and most books on pastoral care do not offer anything beyond the first year.

In his book *Grief, Transition, and Loss: A Pastor's Practical Guide*, Wayne Oates gives an excellent list of modes of caring at the time of a death: "(1) Planning the funeral. . . . (2) The funeral itself. . . . (3) eliciting the family story of the death. . . . (4) developing "'The Story' of a Death". . . . [and] (5) the follow-up."[34]

Eliciting the family story of the death and developing "'The Story of a Death" are wonderful ideas for pastoral care that are spelled out in ways that I have not seen elsewhere. However, the follow-up care suggestions (which include contact at anniversaries and holidays) do not go beyond the first year. An earlier book by Oates has an excellent chapter, "Pastoral Rituals in Grief and Separation," but here again there is nothing suggested for beyond the first year.[35]

All Our Losses, All Our Griefs: Resources for Pastoral Care is a good book on dealing with grief and has a chapter entitled "Toward a Theology for Grieving," but it offers no specifics for after the initial crisis other than an All Saints' Day remembrance.[36] A challenge for the pastor is to lead in the creation of liturgy and rituals to use during and beyond the first year of bereavement, liturgy and rituals that establish and maintain order, affirm and reaffirm meaning, bond community, handle ambivalence, and help people encounter mystery.

Be Familiar with Mourning Rituals

Rituals are the language of the soul; they express what words sometimes cannot; they connect the world around us to the inner world of the self. Because God dwells in that inner world within every person, rituals can connect us to God. Thus ritualization is very much a spiritual experience. A ritual is a specific behavior or activity that gives symbolic expression to specific feelings and thoughts.

Tom F. Driver describes three gifts that rituals offer to social life:

1. The establishment of order
2. The deepening of communal life
3. [Assisting] the dynamic of social change through ritual processes of transformation.[37]

Using the concept of liminality, made prominent by anthropologist Victor Turner, Driver points out that ritual, along with religion and liberative action, constructs "alternate worlds, nourishing themselves with imaginative visions. Different from ordinary life, they move in a kind of liminal space, at the edge of, or in the cracks between, the mapped regions of what we like to call the real world."[38]

During times in our lives when things go fairly smoothly, we may not need many rituals. But in times of difficult transitions, illness, and particularly when mourning the death of a loved one, rituals can become very important and can provide an avenue to healing. Driver says, "Ritual is best understood from a vantage point created by a 'preferential option for the poor,' [saying] we cannot well appreciate the power of ritual unless we see its usefulness to those in need, especially those who having little social power and . . . have a need for the social structure to be transformed."[39] The bereaved are certainly in this category.

Most cultures develop rituals to respond to profound human experiences. Some of these are rites of passage, rituals that surround significant times of transition such as birth, initiation into adulthood, marriage, and death. In "Ritual Responses to Death," Paul E. Irion looks at the needs of grieving as they are addressed by the three stages of rites of passage: separation, transition, and incorporation.[40] This is yet another way to look at the tasks of grief.

Peg Mayo describes "rituals for transmuting grief to creativity." These include creative visualization, meditation, mantras or affirmation, movement, sound (which consists of wailing/keening, weeping, lamenting, sighing, singing, chanting, and toning), creative projection, journaling, dream work, and specific rituals for saying goodbye to the deceased.[41] While these are not specifically Christian, there are many Christian expressions of these rituals.

Rituals can address and help one to process many aspects of grief. However, rituals are not magic. In *Grief, Dying and Death: Clinical Interventions for Caregivers*, Therese Rando points out that the power in rituals "comes from the faith that the individual has in their ability to provide meaning."[42] Rando lists some therapeutic properties of rituals:

•*The power of acting-out.* Acting-out enables the griever to constructively do something to overcome the feelings of emptiness and powerlessness that often accompany bereavement. It gives the individual a sense of control. . . . The physical reality of ritual behavior touches upon the griever's unconscious feelings far more effectively than any words can. . . .

- *The legitimization of emotional and physical ventilation.* Rituals give the mourner permission to outwardly express his feelings, providing acceptable outlets and symbols to focus upon.

- *The delimitation of grief.* Grief can seem overwhelming when it is experienced as a diffuse, global reaction. Ritual can channel feelings of grief into a circumscribed activity having a distinct beginning and ending with a clear purpose, making the feelings more manageable.

- *The opportunity for the bereaved to "hang on" to the deceased without doing so inappropriately or interfering with grief work.* Participation in ritual behaviors may give the griever a chance to interact intensely with the memory of the deceased for a limited period of time without crossing over into pathological dimensions. . . .

- *The provision of assistance in mourning and in confronting unresolved grief.* Rituals allow the griever to state consciously and unconsciously, implicitly and explicitly, that a loss has occurred.

- *The learning gained through doing and experiencing.* Participation in ritual behavior "teaches" the mourner that the deceased is gone. It provides the experience necessary to validate the loss.

- *The provision of structure for ambivalent or nebulous affect and cognition.* Ritualization provides a focus that is especially helpful in managing the confusing disorganization and loss of control commonly experienced in grief.

- *The provision of experiences that may allow for the participation of other group members.* Collective rituals promote the social interaction that is a requisite for successful grief resolution and reintegration into the social group.

•*The structuring of "celebrations" of anniversaries and holidays.* Participation in ritual activities commemorating a special date may provide an unusually effective way of tapping into or confronting a griever's anniversary reactions.[43]

Driver focuses on the transforming power of ritual and includes maxims for the planning of Christian rituals, many of which are particularly useful in thinking about rituals for mourning.

•All rituals invoke powers. A ritual is religious when those powers receive adoration. It is Christian when the powers are God, Christ and Holy Spirit.

•A Christian ritual "works" only when its participants are willing to make demands upon God. ("Ask and you shall receive.")

•The form of a Christian ritual may be very traditional or very innovative or both at once, since form in ritual is nothing but technique, and substance is spirit.

•Christian ritual is liminal and authentic when the people of God receive the spirit of God into their midst.

•The liminality of ritual can be used by God to weaken the grip of oppressive powers. In fact, God has no other use for it.[44]

"The liminality in ritual," says Driver, "is the power of transcendence, of no-saying, of expressing what society and culture deny, of unmasking pretension, of elevating persons and things of 'low degree,' of 'putting down the mighty from their seats' (Luke 1: 52-53)."[45]

In their seminars and books, Dennis, Matthew, and Sheila Fabricant Linn use creative visualization and guided meditation to lead people to places where they experience spiritual, emotional, and psychological healing.[46] These rituals can also be used for grieving situations.

When caregivers understand the importance and power of rituals they can support people in choosing ways to express themselves and mark significant times. North

American cultures have numerous rituals immediately following a death, but there are few defined rituals after the first several weeks. This gives people an opportunity to create their own rituals that have meaning for them. As the first anniversary of Harold's death approached, I contacted a number of widowed friends, collected their stories about marking the first anniversaries of their losses, and then created my own ritual.

James Lapp wrote the story of his grief following the death of his late wife after a prolonged illness with cancer. He ritualized the reality of Nancy's absence in a special service on the first anniversary of her death.

> On the table burned two candles in candleholders used at our wedding thirty-nine years before. To mark the change, I transferred the light from Nancy's candle to a small lamp as a symbol of the different but enduring place she will hold in my life. With great poignancy, Nancy's wedding candle was then snuffed out. My light was transferred to a new candle and candleholder to symbolize a fresh beginning. Then my wedding candle was also extinguished.[47]

Family members and close friends gathered around survey respondent Elizabeth and her children on the first anniversary of her husband's death to plant a tree in his memory. They ate a carry-in meal together and then gathered in the family living room to remember him. Candles burned, and the chair in which he sat during his illness was left empty as a symbol of both his presence and his absence.

Ann went on a retreat on the first anniversary of her spouse's death. She took the cards she had received during the previous year and felt surrounded by love as she reread them.

The first anniversary of the death of Joy's husband coincided with a wedding of a close family friend. Going to weddings was difficult for Joy, as it is for most, if not all, widowed people during the early months after the death of a marriage partner. But she realized that it would have been more difficult not to go. She was with her children, and the day had enough distractions that she managed to get through it, but she was hit by great sadness when she returned home.

Jay and his daughter invited friends to their home to remember their loved one. They used candles and balloons and invited those who came to bring a "colorful symbol of hope" which they shared with the group.

Bonnie, her family, and close friends from church gathered at the cemetery on the anniversary of her husband's death. They gathered around the newly placed stone, and her nephew led in a devotional. Bonnie had taken an armful of long-stemmed roses, and one by one those present took a rose and placed it beside the stone as they shared about Don's impact on their lives and how they had grown from knowing him. On the second anniversary of Don's death, Bonnie put his picture in the newspaper, remembering him "with a smile, a tear, and love."

June told me that she had invited friends to join her on the first anniversary of her husband's death. However, nothing specific was planned, and she found the time together awkward. She advised me to plan ahead for what I needed and wanted to happen.

I invited family and friends "who are not afraid to weep or walk with those who weep" (as I put it in the invitation) to join me on the first anniversary of Harold's death. We gathered without speaking in my home, listening to the music of piano, violin, and recorder playing hymns that had helped to sustain me in the previous months. We then walked in silence on the path along the canal where Harold had had a heart attack and died instantly one year earlier. Walking along that path where his spirit left his body was difficult for me, but that evening I felt upheld by the fifty people who, like a great cloud, silently cheered me on with their presence. A blue heron escorted us for part of the two-mile walk, repeatedly lighting on the water of the canal and then lifting into the moonlit darkening sky. This was an unexpected gift, a reminder to me of God's eternal presence. The blue heron was indeed a symbol of hope and of the unexpected gifts I received on my journey. Words were not spoken on this walk because they were not necessary.

These stories may prompt more ideas of ways to mark anniversary dates that can be tailored to individual situations. Many people find reading about grief, especially other grief stories, to be a kind of ritual. Others' stories help to normalize the feelings and behaviors of grief. In addition, they can be a way to meet God; recognizing God at work in another person's life can open awareness to how God is working in one's own life.

It is important to remember that explicit rituals are resources that some people will choose, not requirements to be imposed. Each person must discover what works for him or her.

Learn from Bereaved People

The best teachers about loss and grief are bereaved people themselves. Reviewing studies of widowed people, listening to people's feelings, questions, and stories, and paying attention to how God is at work in the lives of suffering people are ways to gain more understanding and become a more helpful friend and caregiver for those whose spouses have died.

Responses to the Living Well questionnaire yield significant information about the sources of important support, about what is helpful after spousal death, about what is not helpful, about how people have been supported by their church families, and about the range of comparisons widowed people make between the first and second year after spousal death.

Sources of Support Following the Death of a Spouse

Two questions about the sources of support were asked: "From where (or from whom) did your most important support come in the first months after your spouse's death?" and "Did that experience of support change after the first year of being widowed?"[48]

One man articulated, "I needed faithful and consistent

friends who were there to be friends, not therapists or anything else. When someone loses a spouse, that person feels peculiar and different. He or she needs at least a few people who in effect say, 'I want to be with you because of who you are, not because of how I can fix you. I value you for your own sake.'"

Eighty-eight percent of those who responded to these questions said that family provided them important support after the death. Sixty percent of the respondents said support came from church family members, while 36 percent said support came from the pastor or pastors. Most of these respondents also indicated that church family members were important to them. However, the options presented on the questionnaire might have skewed this data. It may be that pastor support is even higher, in that some respondents may have included "pastor" in "church family members" or in "longtime friends."

A desire for pastoral visits was cited by numerous people, some who wanted more visits and some who didn't have any visits. The most dramatic case I heard about was from a couple who were very active in an Anabaptist congregation. He had been the choir director and served on the church board. She had served as a Sunday school teacher and as the church secretary. When a sudden death devastated this household, the pastor did not visit one time. The couple left the church and years later remember the pain of the pastoral negligence.[49]

Sixty percent said that longtime friends offered important support. Many of these were the same who checked "church family members." In some cases these likely refer to the same individuals giving support to the bereaved.

Thirty percent indicated that widowed people gave important support. A few said funeral home personnel were supportive. Also mentioned as supportive were in-laws, neighbors, work colleagues, hospice personnel, new friends, grandchildren, and God. It was mentioned a few times that family members were so grief-stricken that they could not provide much support initially.

Fortunately all the respondents indicated that they had some important support.

Changes in Support After the First Year

Some respondents said that their experiences of support did *not* change after the first year, implying that the support was ongoing. Others said that the support *did* change. Those responses fell into four general categories. Some indicated that they understood why the changes in support occurred and they were not unhappy about it. For example, one wrote, "I had fewer calls and visits [after the first year], which was understandable and natural." Another wrote, "Others needed that attention; I did not feel neglected." In contrast, a second group of respondents seemed to feel neglected and unhappy about the change in support. One wrote, "Some 'so-called' friends seemed to disappear as time went by while others supported me. Another responded, "People forget. They left me on my own." A third group simply reported the changes factually with little indication of their response to it. For example, one person answered, "Support was less intentional. Active support gradually diminished." A smaller number of respondents mentioned moving into new relationships, which changed their need (or apparent need) for support. An example of these is the man who wrote, "I got remarried eighteen months after my wife's death and thus it was assumed I was all 'healed.'"

Helpful Things After Spousal Death

Many responses were given to the question "What were some of the most helpful things that happened to you or were provided for you during the first months after you spouse's death?" Many mentioned support from their church, church family, and church friends, naming many invitations and various kinds of emotional and tangible support. Others described the prayers of others and their own spiritual beliefs as among the most helpful things provided them. Many named the presence of family or friends in response to this question and elaborated on specific occasions or commitments. For example, one woman wrote, "Family stayed for a week; two of my children helped me go through all his things." Some described the accepting quality of this presence, for example, "Frequent dinner invitations from a couple who had been friends with us both and who gave me an opportunity to talk without the need to edit what I said." It is clear that people want compassion more than they want sympathy.

What *Not* to Say When Someone's Spouse Dies

While I prefer to focus on the positive, I did include a rather negative question in my questionnaire. Because I have heard many stories of disturbing and hurtful things that have been said to bereaved people, and because I believe that usually people do not intend to be hurtful, I asked the question "If you were to write an article or book entitled, 'What NOT to Say When Someone's Spouse Dies,' what would it include?" (Readers who may have said things described below are encouraged not to feel guilty, but rather are invited to be more thoughtful in the future.)

A large majority of the respondents, 79 percent, answered this question. Some people described positive responses, even to potentially hurtful comments. One wrote,

> I was blessed with so many friends and family members who surrounded me during the viewing, funeral, burial and later with letters, cards, calls and emails. Some were refined, some cold, some warm, some unpolished, some loving, but each one was very special to me. I understood what they wanted to say. It was difficult for many people to talk to me because not everyone has the best command of words at a time like this. I can truly say that I appreciated everyone that was willing to come and talk. I remember the many people who talked to me and remembered positive things about my husband, but I do not remember of being offended or hurt by anything said. It was impressive and inspiring just to have people be with me and share the sorrow.

Other responses included "I didn't have any bad experiences in this way" and "Most people were kind in their comments." Others wrote,

I was simply glad if people would say something and felt very ready to forgive if something not quite "right" was said—because I always felt/feel awkward and afraid to say the wrong thing when I talk to a grieving person. I would make my main focus the fact that saying something is not essential or particularly helpful. Presence and acts of kindness after the funeral are much more important than "words."

Just a hug and "I'm praying for you" means so much more than reciting a Bible verse. I did not have negative feelings toward any remarks because I knew they were given with deep concern and wanting to be supportive even though some were not that helpful. What I found least helpful was assumptions that were made about what I needed. I wasn't too aware of what people said.

Along the same line, one respondent said, "I wouldn't write such an article. I'm sure there were occasions when expressions of sympathy were worded inappropriately but I don't remember them." Two people remembered negative comments as an afterthought: "Nobody said anything hurtful or inappropriate. Well, maybe once . . ." and "I don't remember getting insensitive comments from people, (although) I guess one might be . . ."

One thoughtful person said, "I do not have any negative thoughts of how people related to me at this time. I took people's comments as an expression of their love and concern for me at a very difficult time. People can only relate out of their own experiences."

These comments offer an important perspective to help balance the negative responses that follow. In spite of these many negative comments, most of these respondents noted that important support came from family, church family, friends, and others.

Trying to remove a bereaved person's grief in the name of faith can be cruel. The religious clichés that are sometimes offered may be facts, but not helpful statements to make when an untimely death has occurred. Yes, a suffering person no longer suffers after death has come, and yes, it could be worse, but being told these things is not comforting. Neither does comfort come with comments about God's will or paltry explanations for the death.

I identified other responses to my question that expressed, in a variety of ways, the idea "Do not ask me how I am unless you really want to know." Seventeen percent indicated they did not like being asked, "How are you?" or "How are you doing?" One person articulated the feelings evoked by the question "Almost everyone is 'sizing up' the survivor as to how he or she is doing. It's as if people are trying to figure out the survivor's level of love for the one who died by how much grief he/she is showing."

When people asked me, "How are you?" I wanted to say, "Do you really want to know, or are you just greeting me?" Sometimes I responded with, "How much time do you have?" In many cultures "How are you?" is a standard greeting. And the expected response is, "Fine." But I am not fine. Years ago I often said I was fine, especially if nobody in the family was sick and my husband brought me flowers and the children washed the dishes without complaining. But then something changed. I had a small taste of suffering and I can no longer ignore the fact that flowers do not grow where bombs explode and starving people do not need to wash dishes. I mourn with the mothers whose sons will not come home and the children who will never know their fathers. I grieve with the parents who do not have food for their children. At times I feel like I will never be fine again.

Eventually I learned to say, "Good morning," or "Good evening," in response to "How are you?" because I knew it was usually just a greeting. After a few years I started saying, "I am well," if indeed I was feeling well. Not "fine"—as though I had no cares in the world—but "well," in that I am facing the challenges in front of me and finding the resources to go on. I would like to change the way we greet each other, but I probably cannot. And a very embarrassing and humbling fact is that I now sometimes ask that question when I do not really mean it.

A number of respondents listed "I know how you feel" as something they did not want to be told. One said, "Nobody knows how you feel. Perhaps they can relate to your feelings, but they can't *know*."

Twenty-six percent of those who responded to this question expressed that it was *not* helpful to hear statements about God's will or that God "needed" the loved one. Similar unhelpful statements mentioned were "God knows best" and "It was God's plan." One person wrote about such statements, "My peace of mind comes from knowing God is with me and grieves with me. It does not come from saying that what happened was God's will!"

Some stated that they did not want to be told that the loved one was better off. From reading the responses to this question in addition to reading and listening to experiences of others, I agree with this statement from one respondent: "In a premature death, any statement that indicated God caused the event to happen would be unwelcome, as well as any statement indicating the hardships awaiting the bereaved."

Some respondents named specific inconsiderate statements or questions they had received, for example, "It could be worse," or "She looks so natural." Others mentioned that they did not want to be told how good they have it or to have their sadness belittled or minimized. Some stated that they did not want explanations for the death, such as the loved one's sin, or "This happened to you because you're strong enough to handle it." Six respondents mentioned that they did not appreciate being told that they were strong. Fourteen people wrote that they did not want to hear that they would (or should) marry again, as though remarriage would make everything better. A group of respondents named various predictions about their future they had heard as unhelpful remarks, such as

"You will have a lot of lonely days; the second year is the worst" or "Time will heal." Another type of unhelpful response mentioned was giving advice. One respondent wrote, "Let me decide when to give away clothes, etc." Another similar response was, "Don't say, 'You've just got to get over your grief.'"

One typical discussion among widows centers on the inappropriateness of the offer to "Let me know if there is anything I can do." In our culture it is difficult to ask for help. When we are mourning and vulnerable and already needing to do so many demanding tasks, *asking* for help is too difficult for many people. *Accepting* help is much easier if it is offered. One bold widow, assuming the offers were genuine, said she responded with "Yes, as a matter of fact, there is something you can do." It soon became apparent that the offer was not for "anything I can do," but rather for "some things that will fit into my schedule." That made it extremely difficult to ask for help again. Much better is the offer to do specific things, such as

•I can help with childcare on Tuesdays, or
•I am available on Wednesday afternoons to help with outdoor work or to get groceries for you, or
•Call me any evening between 6 p.m. and 11 p.m.

Messages to the Church Family

The Living Well questionnaire asked, "What messages, both the positive and the negative, did you give (or would you like to have given) to your church family about those early weeks and months?" This question had responses from 131 people, and far more of these were positive than negative. At least fifty people felt support from their church and expressed appreciation and compliments. Some specifically noted appreciation for prayer support. One group of responses expressed a need similar to this: "I would say just spend time with me, talk with me, cry with me, be my support." Twelve people expressed the desire for church people to remember them. Many people responded that they would like to tell the church to be more inclusive. Another group of responses expressed the wish that others try to understand them. Fourteen people specifically asked for others to keep talking about the deceased spouse. Five would encourage people not to be "afraid" to talk about him or her. At least fourteen people expressed needing or wanting more attention and pastoral care than they received.

A related question was, "What messages did you give (or would you like to have given) to your church family about your experiences and needs *after* the first year of widowhood?" The responses to this question were much the same as to the above question, including asking for ongoing support. One respondent wrote, "I am still hurting deeply. I'm not doing as well as you think I am." Some stated a variation of "Please keep talking about my spouse; I want to still hear his or her name." Others asked to be included and treated like "normal," or said in some way, "Please keep in touch with me." Still others want their church families to continue to be sensitive to their situations, including the dilemma of being a single person in a couples' world. Many expressed deep appreciation and gratitude for all the love, support, and compassion they had received from the church.

Some said they needed space, saying they got tired of answering the question, "How are you doing?" The contrast between people wanting more care and others wanting less is an example of the great challenge of relating to widowed people. Many would agree with these statements: "We cannot be pleased. We are not happy if you say something and we are not happy if you say nothing. The fact is that nothing can make us happy at this time. This is a very difficult time. So do not take our disappointments or our criticisms personally. Hang in there with us and eventually life will be better for us."

There are numerous published sources that include lists of what is helpful for friends and other caregivers to offer to bereaved people. One concise list written in the context of author Sara Wengerd's personal story is *A F Grief: Walking with Your Friend Through Loss.* especially to the last three chapters, "Changes," ᴛʜᴇ Second Year," and "Adjustment," which list practical ideas of how to offer ongoing support.[50] Another widow interviewed many bereaved people and compiled her findings in *Don't Ask for a Dead Man's Golf Clubs.*[51] This book includes quotations from survivors about helpful things at the time of death, helpful things later, and unhelpful things they were offered after the death. Both of these books offer information consistent with the data gathered in the Living Well study.

A Plan for Pastoral Care for Bereaved Widowed People

Most pastors know and follow effective roles at the time of a death, especially when the deceased is a parishioner. Presence and prayer are important to many people, even those who do not regularly pray or attend church, and pastors are often invited to provide that.

Suggestions for pastoral care for the short term can be found in the guidelines established by Neuger for pastoral counseling. These include using an approach that is reasonably short-term, involving resources from within the congregation and community, and maintaining boundaries between pastoral counseling and other pastoral roles.[52]

Beyond the days of the death, family visitation, funeral or memorial service, and the disposal of the body, there are fewer guidelines for pastoral care of the bereaved. Keeping in mind that ministry is actually an art, a pastoral caregiver continually discerns the best role to take at specific times. Sometimes the caregiver needs to be a companion, sometimes a guide, sometimes a comforter. Flexibility is essential. As with pastoral care for all types of individuals, the way of wisdom is to listen more than to speak, to give advice sparingly, to respect silence, and to always respect confidentiality.

Additional helpful guidelines exist for working specifically with bereaved people. Zisook and Shuchter outline six noteworthy therapeutic tasks of grief following the death of a spouse. These are "used as operational definitions" of an "optimal outcome."

1. Development of the capacity to experience, express, and integrate painful affects;
2. Utilization of the most adaptive means of modulating painful affects;
3. Integration of the continuing relationship with the dead spouse;
4. Maintenance of health and continued functioning;
5. Achievement of a successful reconfiguration of altered relationships;
6. Achievement of an integrated, healthy self-concept and stable worldview.[53]

Following is a list I have developed of activities that can be carried out by pastors, other leaders, and volunteers within a congregation to minister to widowed people and their families. Many of these are not only for widowed people; they may be useful for people who grieve the deaths of other loved ones. Also, many of the following tasks can be enacted by any loving person. The church is, after all, a priesthood of believers.

1. Pray for bereaved people and assure them of your prayers. This support includes private prayers and prayers during corporate worship.
2. Maintain weekly contact for the first two months by a person who represents the church.
3. Maintain monthly contact for the remainder of the first year by a person who represents the church and regular contact into the second and third years. This should be continued even for widowed people who become involved in another relationship, because the grief for the lost partner does not end when a new relationship begins.
4. Enter into the grief of a bereaved person as a compassionate observer who may also lament

and who interprets the "lived experience of death as an opportunity for the soul to find deeper meaning in God."[54]

5. Pastors should lead the entire congregation, including those who are not bereaved (because they likely will be bereaved someday), in corporate laments and promote the concept that death and resurrection are part of the normal cycles of life and not to be feared or avoided. This can be done in sermons and in pastoral care.

6. Similarly, pastors are called to lead the community of faith in its two-fold role that enables the movement from lament to praise: (1) standing in solidarity with those who suffer, and (2) offering God's healing presence to them. This is called for in the funeral or memorial service *and* beyond.

7. Offer information about grief and mourning. This can take place in many ways, but the pastoral staff of a church should ensure that bereaved people are aware of the many aspects of grief that are normal, but sometimes disturbing or frightening.

8. Assist the bereaved in understanding some important concepts:
   - God's love is bigger than any loss.
   - God is always present in our lives, even when the presence is not felt.
   - Each person and each situation is unique; there are many ways to mourn.
   - Symbols and rituals are the language of the soul, useful when words are not adequate.
   - Sorrow and joy are interconnected.
   - Recognize the time of bereavement following the death of a spouse as a phase of the marriage, one that requires time and attention different from, but perhaps not less important than, earlier phases of the marriage.

9. Provide a variety of books on grief in the church library. (See the annotated bibliography of books for bereaved—particularly widowed— people at the end of this book.)

10. Offer literature as a gift from the congregation. Two excellent options are included at the end of the annotated bibliography.

11. Consider starting support groups for bereaved people within the congregation or community, or assist, if necessary, the bereaved in getting into an existing support group.

12. Offer grief counseling for the bereaved (including children), either by the pastoral staff or professional counselors, paying for counseling if appropriate.

13. Suggest that the bereaved person consider meeting with a spiritual director or offer to pay for tuition for classes in spirituality for those who would like that kind of help in growing spiritually, remembering that liminal spaces are ripe for soul-awakening.

14. Invite bereaved people to tell their stories in settings appropriate for each individual, such as Sunday school classes or fellowship night programs. For people who cannot or do not want to speak publicly, reading Scripture, singing in the choir, sharing artwork, or being a participant—even a silent participant—in a drama might be other ways to "tell the story" in the congregational setting.

15. Plan an All Saints' Day or Eternity Sunday observance.[55] Consider remembering the deceased members of the community for at least two years. One way to be inclusive of all people in the congregation who grieve the deaths of loved ones is to invite members to submit names of loved ones they would like to have remembered. The remembrances can be expressed in various

ways: the person can be named, a candle can be lit in his or her memory, or a brief statement about each person can be presented in verbal or written form.[56]

16. Offer to help plan a service on the first anniversary of the death of the beloved. There is no limit to the meaningful rituals and symbols that might be used to assist in grieving and growing, and many people will benefit from developing a plan that expresses themselves. However, other grieving people may not have the time, energy, or wherewithal to plan a service. For these people, members of the congregation can provide great assistance in helping to develop a plan for a service in memory of the deceased.

17. Plan special services or occasions of blessing for widowed people according to need and interest. Two samples are in *Minister's Manual*, one specifically for widowhood[57] and one as a blessing for those who choose a life of celibacy, either for a limited time or for a lifetime.[58]

18. Encourage bereaved people to be involved in congregational life to help promote positive connections with others. Loneliness rarely comes from being alone. As Kropf said, "It comes from not being connected with others in ways that make us feel safe, understood, and cared for."[59]

19. Encourage people in the congregation to invite bereaved people to sit with them during church and regularly inquire of the bereaved person as to how he or she is managing in coming to church without a spouse.

20. As bereaved people experience transformation, grow spiritually and make discoveries, encourage and support them in using their gifts within the congregation.

Being an expert on grief is not necessary for effective pastoral work with grieving people. Pastoral care is God's work. Pastors join in God's work in the world when they listen to what grieving people are saying, listen to the voice of God within themselves, and then with the guidance of the Holy Spirit respond using good communication skills. The answers for many of life's questions are within the people asking the questions. Pastoral care includes helping people listen to that inner voice of God. Rabbi Earl Grollman writes,

> The pastor is most effective when he acts as a pastor, not as an amateur psychiatrist. He should not forsake his own traditional resources and spiritual functions. His is a fellowship with a past, a present, and a future tied together by rites, theology and a religious ethic. He has his own unique framework of viewing and handling guilt, forgiveness, conflict, suffering and hostility.[60]

Most important, all that ministering people do must be rooted and grounded in prayer and compassion. Walking with a person on a grief journey is indeed sacred work. It can be an opportunity to participate in the process of holy transformation as a bereaved person finds self-expression in laments, learns new truths about God, the self, and the world, and discovers hope within the struggle to find new life.

Encouraging and participating in rituals that nurture spirituality are ways that an entire congregation can assist those who mourn. For a bereaved person to move toward healing following the death of a loved one, it is necessary to walk into the darkness, embrace the grief, and feel the pain deep within. This can be done effectively with the use of rituals and symbols. Surrounded by a loving congregation, those who mourn will feel God's presence and can therein find the courage and the strength to move along on the journey in grief.

Conclusion

[God] did not say: You will not be troubled,
you will not be belabored, you will not be disquieted;
but he said: You will not be overcome.
God wants us to pay attention to these words,
and always to be strong in faithful trust,
in well-being and in woe,
for he loves us and delights in us,
and so he wishes us to love him and delight in him
and trust greatly in him,
and all will be well.
—Julian of Norwich[1]

"And all will be well." I am well. There are times when I feel fine, but it is hard to feel fine when there is so much violence, suffering, and death in this world. *Well* has much deeper roots than *fine*. Fine is a superficial thing, and I am well even when I am not fine. Well comes with the assurance that God is love and God is with us even in the face of devastation, loss, and suffering that seems overwhelming.

A powerful vision of God's gracious, sustaining, unfailing love comes to us from Julian of Norwich. Julian, a remarkable fourteenth-century woman who lived as an anchoress in the English cathedral city of Norwich, is the best known of the English medieval mystics and is considered by some to be the most perceptive Christian of the second millennium. Her *Revelations of Divine Love* is a theological treatise that is an extraordinary record of a medieval religious experience. It is remarkable because of the author's profound understanding of the Christian mysteries, for the deep understanding of her own experience, and for the conviction, intelligence, and beauty in the way she expresses herself. Julian offers us a treatise on an alternate way of "knowing."

Medieval English scholar Grace Jantzen is struck by the frequency with which Julian uses the vocabulary of "desire." Julian's spirituality is permeated with desire for God.[2] Hers is a spirituality that is contagious in her eloquent writings about God's love, longing for God, and human suffering.

Julian's writings are animated by a mature and profound Christian hope. Her hope is challenged by her awareness of her own sin and by the presence of sin, evil, and suffering in the world. Nevertheless, she has an amazing and unquenchable optimism. Throughout *Revelations* are words animated with effervescent hope: "and all will be well."

In 2002 I went to Norwich and visited Julian's cell, the small room attached to the church where she lived her religious vocation of a nearly solitary life. It was a pivotal point on my journey of grief and transformation. For years I had struggled for an appropriate response to the persistent greeting, "How are you?" In that ancient holy place, brimming with goodness and optimism that could come only from God, I realized I was well.

I began writing my master's thesis project in 2003, believing that loss is an invitation to transformation and that one could live well following the death of a spouse. My study of loss and grief, spiritual formation, and human development; the responses to my empirical inquiry; and my personal experiences and reflections have led to the conclusion that all people suffer loss, that loss comes with an invitation that can be either accepted or rejected, and that transformation is an ongoing gift of God. In this process I have established or confirmed the following:

1. Everyone suffers significant personal loss.
2. We need to mourn our losses.

3. Lament as outlined and illustrated in biblical laments is an effective way to mourn.
4. Our great losses are with us forever in our conscious or unconscious memories, shaping who we are and how we view the world.
5. We can learn to integrate losses into our lives so that we can live well following the death of a spouse or other loved one.
6. There are gifts in grief.
7. Suffering opens possibilities for greater joy in life.
8. Losing a spouse in death is not necessarily the worst kind of loss, but it is unique in the ways that sexuality and identity are involved.
9. There are practical and effective ways for celibate people to deal with sexual energy.
10. Pastoral care needs for widowed people may go on indefinitely.

The best way to respond to loss is to enter into the process of transformation. That process includes lamenting, allowing the pain of loss to touch the core of one's being and expressing that pain with anguish and perhaps with accusations and anger; learning about the paradoxes of joy and sorrow, of life and death, and of suffering and transformation; and emerging from the "dark night" with a new identity and renewed hope. One does not forget the loss, but is transformed by the love of God while struggling with the loss within the care of a community of believers. Living well is knowing that joy and sorrow are inseparable. Living well is *not* living without suffering or pain. It is realizing that life will bring challenges, yet being at peace, knowing that the God who loves us more than we can imagine is always present with us. Living well is recognizing suffering as an opportunity for life-changing and life-giving growth.

Appendix

The Living Well Questionnaire

1121 South Main Street
Goshen, IN 46526
January 2004

Dear Friends and acquaintances who are (or at one time were) widowed,

I am a student at Associated Mennonite Biblical Seminary where I am writing a thesis as part of my requirement for a master of arts in Christian formation degree. The title is "Loss as an Invitation to Transformation: Living Well Following the Death of a Spouse."

I invite you to participate in my research by completing the enclosed questionnaire. The primary purposes of this study are:

1. To try to "normalize" grief. All grieve differently. I want to confirm the wide range of what is normal and then make the findings available to people who are grieving and to caregivers.
2. To identify some healthy ways to respond to loss and to process grief.
3. To offer caregivers (pastors, counselors, family members

and friends) a better grounded understanding of the needs, experiences, struggles, and thoughts of widowed people so that they can be more supportive.
4. To find answers to some of my questions that remain more than four years after the sudden death of my husband.

There are many resources available for coping with grief in the early months following the death of a spouse. However, I have found fewer resources related to the second, third, and fourth years of widowhood and beyond. In addition to information in the literature, I want to take a fresh look at the stories of people who "have been there." Together we can help those who have not walked in our shoes to better understand us and to more effectively support widowed people.

Because some questions are very personal, I have arranged for you to return the questionnaire in such a way that you can remain anonymous. The return envelope is addressed to Dr. Daniel Schipani, my AMBS Faculty Advisor, who will remove the responses from the envelopes (so that I will not see the postmark) before giving them to me. Although I am sending out approximately 200 questionnaires, I may have some hunches about the identity of some respondents, so in addition, I assure you that your information will be treated with the greatest confidentiality.

Some people receiving this questionnaire have been widowed more than once. If you are one of those, I invite you to answer the questions with adaptations or while thinking of one of your late spouses. If you care to make comparisons, I will value the information.

Thank you in advance for participating in this study. May you know and feel God's blessing, wherever you are on life's journey.

Sincerely,
Rachel Nafziger Hartzler

Living Well After the Death of a Spouse Questionnaire[3]

YOUR RESPONSES WILL BE VALUABLE
EVEN IF YOU SKIP OVER SOME QUESTIONS OR GIVE
BRIEF ANSWERS

In the first ten questions you are asked to recall the time soon after your spouse's death and to make some comparisons.

1. How long ago did your spouse die?
   ___ within the past year
   ___ between one to two years ago
   ___ between two and three years ago
   ___ between three and four years ago
   ___ between four and five years ago
   ___ between five and ten years ago
   ___ between ten and twenty years ago
   ___ more than twenty years ago

2. What were your most <u>difficult</u> tasks during the first months after the death of your spouse?

3. What were some of the most <u>helpful</u> things that happened to you or were provided for you during those first months?

4. From where (or from whom) did your most important support come in the first months after your spouse's death? *(check more than one if applicable)*
   ___ family members   ___ church family members
   ___ parents   ___ longtime friends
   ___ siblings   ___ widowed people
   ___ children   ___ funeral home personnel
   ___ pastor(s)   ___ others *(Please specify)*

5. Did that experience of support change after the first year of being widowed? ___ Yes ___ No. If so, how?

6. What did you miss most about your spouse in the first months after the death? *(If you are inclined to check several of the following, prioritize or rate them as 1, 2, 3 . . . with #1 being "what I missed the most.")*
___ my spouse's overall companionship
___ my spouse's physical presence
___ our emotional intimacy
___ our sexual intimacy
___ our physical (but not necessarily sexual) intimacy
___ other

7. Are there ways that what you missed most about your spouse changed after the first several months? ___Yes ___ No. If so, can you identify those?

8. If you were to write an article or book entitled "What NOT to Say When Someone's Spouse Dies," what would it include?!

9. How did your spouse's death affect your relationship with God?

Has your relationship with God continued to change?

10. What messages did you give (or would you like to have given) to your church family about those early weeks and months— both the positive and the negative?

Questions 11 through 17 ask you to reflect on the ongoing tasks of widowhood. You may skip any questions which do not pertain to you.

11. What messages did you give (or would you like to have given) to your church family about your experiences and needs <u>after the first year of widowhood</u>—both the positive and the negative?

12. If it has been more than one year since your spouse's death, how is or was the second year different from the first?
    ___ easier because . . .
    ___ more difficult because . . .
    ___ not much different
    ___ I can't remember!
    ___ not necessarily easier or more difficult, but different in the following ways:

13. Of course we will never forget our deceased spouses; in some ways we will never "get over it." However, have you been able to separate yourself from your deceased spouse so that grief is not the major theme of your life? ___ Yes ___ No

    If so, when did that happen in relation to the death?
    ___ in less than one year; if so, how many months? ___
    ___ at about one year after the death
    ___ at about two years
    ___ at about three years
    ___ at about four years
    ___ at about five years
    ___ more than five years; if so, approximately how many years? ___

14. What would you say is the major task or agenda of grief following the death of a spouse? How did you work (or are you working) at the major task(s) of grief?

15. Many bereaved people eventually find a gift or gifts in grief. Have you experienced some gift(s) that you can name?

16. Since your spouse's death, what observations have you made about the way others relate to you, such as, have you been told directly (or indirectly) that you should be "over it"? If so, how do you respond?

17. If you have experienced an attraction to or interest in a person(s) of the opposite gender:

    a. When did this first occur in relation to the death of your late spouse?
    ___ within the first 3 months   ___ between 12 and 18 months
    ___ between 3 and 6 months   ___ between 18 and 24 months
    ___ between 6 and 9 months   ___ between 2 and 3 years
    ___ between 9 and 12 months ___ other _____

    b. How did you feel when this happened? *(check as many as apply)*
    ___ startled   ___ ready for another relationship
    ___ frightened   ___ not ready for another relationship
    ___ confused   ___ other _____
    ___ delighted

    c. How did (or do) you manage/respond to those feelings?

"Relationship" in the following questions refers to a romantic involvement with a person of the opposite gender. Remember that you will return the questionnaire in such a way that the researcher will not see the postmark—so your responses will be anonymous. If you have not dated/courted/spent time with a person of the opposite gender you may skip to question 24.

18. **If you dated/courted/spent time with a person of the opposite gender:**

    a. When did this <u>first</u> occur in relation to the death of your spouse?
    ___ within the first 3 months ___ between 12 and 18 months
    ___ between 3 and 6 months ___ between 18 and 24 months
    ___ between 6 and 9 months ___ between 2 and 3 years
    ___ between 9 and 12 months ___ other _____

    b. What happened to this <u>first</u> relationship?
    ___ it ended after ____ time(s) together or
    ___ it ended after ____ months or ____ years
    ___ it led to marriage after ____ months or ____ years
    ___ the relationship is continuing
    ___ other:

    c. What is/was the marital status of the other person?
    ___ never married   ___ widowed   ___ divorced

19. **Have other significant relationships occurred for you?**
    ___Yes   ___ No
    a. If so, how many? ____
    b. How long did each last? ____

20. **If you are currently in a relationship (other than the first one)**

    a. When did this relationship begin in relation to the death of your spouse?
    ___ within the first 3 months ___ between 12 and 18 months
    ___ between 3 and 6 months ___ between 18 and 24 months
    ___ between 6 and 9 months ___ between 2 and 3 years
    ___ between 9 and 12 months ___ other _____

  b. What is the status of this relationship?
  ___ we are married
  ___ we plan to be married
  ___ we plan to remain friends but not marry
  ___ we have made no commitments

  c. What is/was the marital status of the other person?
  ___ divorced
  ___ never married
  ___ widowed

21. What regrets (if any) do you have about relationships in which you have been involved?

22. What would you do differently if you were starting over in the dating process, or what advice would you give (regarding dating) to a recently widowed person?

23. If you have remarried:

  a. Have you continued to grieve the death of your deceased spouse within the context of your new marriage? If so, how have you managed that?

  b. What are some of the ways in which this marriage is different from your previous marriage(s)?

  c. In light of your own experience, what advice regarding marriage would you give to widowed people who have not remarried?

24. Are there ways in which you have confused your deceased spouse and another person(s) to whom you have been attracted or with whom you have had a relationship?

If so, what have you learned about yourself and/or the grief process?

25. What has happened to other friendships since you have been widowed?

Some of the possibilities may follow here and on the next page. If you have had experiences in addition to (or other than) these, please list them.

a. Of the "couple friends" we had <u>before</u> my spouse's death, the following have stood beside me: *(check one)*

____ all my friends   ____ only a few friends
____ most friends   ____ none of my former friends
____ some friends

I think it may be because:

As a result, I have felt:

b. My relationships with single friends have changed in the following ways: *(check as many as apply)*
___ I have more single friends
___ Most of my single friends are widowed
___ Most of my widowed friends are of the same gender
___ I am cautious in relating to single friends of the opposite gender because of:
___ the possibility of giving the "wrong" impression
___ other:

c. **I have** *(delete those that do not apply)* **many, a few, no <u>new</u> friends.**

I would describe my new friends in the following ways:
(check as many as apply)

___ widowed	___ from my work setting
___ never married	___ from a grief group
___ divorced	___ married and of both genders
___ close to my age	___ married and of the same gender
___ of all age groups	___ married and of the opposite gender
___ from my church	___ other

d. **Other experiences with friends during widowhood:**

The following three questions are related to celibate sexuality.

26. **Adults have varying degrees of sexual longings that may or may not change after being widowed. What changes, if any, have you experienced?**

27. **If you have been celibate for periods of time, what have you done (or do you do) with your sexual energy?** *(check as many as apply)*

    ___ I have tried to deny it by staying busy

    ___ I have tried to transfer this energy into wholesome activities such as:

    ___ I have engaged in self-pleasuring or masturbation

    ___ I have used it as an opportunity to learn about myself

    ___ I have talked about it with close friends

    ___ I have remained frustrated

    ___ other

    ___ I would welcome literature about healthy celibate living for sexual people.

28. Some experts encourage widowed people to masturbate. A few claim that it is impossible to fantasize about a deceased spouse while masturbating. If you masturbate(d), whom do/did you fantasize or think about at that time?

___ my deceased spouse   ___ a nonspecific other person
___ a specific other person   ___ other

Please answer the following about yourself:

29. Gender: ___ female ___ male

Age when first widowed: ___ under 40   ___ 40 to 49
    ___ 50 to 59   ___ 60 to 69
    ___ 70 to 79   ___ 80 or over

Present age: ___ under 40   ___ 40 to 49   ___ 50 to 59
    ___ 60 to 69   ___ 70 to 79   ___ 80 or over

Church affiliation (denomination only)

_____

30. How long were you married to your spouse(s) before his/her death? ___ years

Any additional comments will be appreciated either here or on another page.

Thank you very much for completing this questionnaire. Your responses will help guide my writing.

Rachel Nafziger Hartzler
December 2003

Annotated Bibliography and Additional Resources

Bell, John L. *The Last Journey: Reflections for the Time of Grieving.* Chicago: GIA Publications, 1996.

> A member of the Iona Community in Scotland, Bell has gathered Scripture, prayers, and poetry into a gift book. Includes an audio recording of Bell's poetry, set to music and sung by the Cathedral Singers of Chicago.

Brothers, Dr. Joyce. *Widowed.* New York: Simon & Schuster, 1990.

> A popular psychologist and author shares her feelings of being lost after the death of her husband and tells how she came to embrace life again. She candidly discusses many issues, including sexuality.

*Chittister, Joan D. *Scarred by Struggle, Transformed by Hope.* Grand Rapids, Mich.: Eerdmans, 2003.

> Referring to the struggle of Jacob with the nocturnal being, Chittister says that authentic hope is born of pain and struggling. "There is only one way out of the struggle and that is by going into the darkness, waiting for the light and being open to new growth. Darkness is the call to faith."

Edelman, Hope. *Motherless Daughters.* New York: Dell Publishing, 1994.

> A motherless daughter since the age of seventeen, Edelman identifies the questions and profound changes women who lose mothers at any age experience, but

especially when they are young. Based on hundreds of interviews, this work was a *New York Times* bestseller.

Ericsson, Stephanie. *Companion through the Darkness: Inner Dialogues on Grief.* New York: HarperCollins, 1993.
An outstanding story of one woman's journey as a widow. Poetic and expressive of feelings and experiences for which some people have difficulty finding words.

Felber, Marta. *Finding Your Way After Your Spouse Dies.* Notre Dame, Ind.: Ave Maria Press, 2000.
Gentle suggestions for widowed people that encourage facing the pain, embracing the grief, and moving forward with life. Each of the sixty-four brief chapters includes a prayer and appropriate Scripture passages for reflection.

———. *Grief Expressed: When a Mate Dies.* West Fork, Ark.: LifeWords, 1997.
A beautiful workbook for newly widowed people woven with Felber's own experience and very practical suggestions.

*Feinberg. Linda. *I'm Grieving as Fast as I Can: How Young Widows and Widowers Can Cope and Heal.* New Horizon Press, 1994.
Writing specifically for widowed people under fifty, Feinberg recognizes some of the unique issues and needs that young widowed people face, especially if they have children at home.

Fitzgerald, Helen. *The Mourning Handbook.* New York: Simon & Schuster, 1994.
A therapist and certified death educator who has grieved the death of a husband has compiled a comprehensive and practical resource for the bereaved.

*Ginsburg, Genevieve Davis. *Widow to Widow: Thoughtful, Practical Ideas for Rebuilding Your Life.* Tucson, Ariz.: Fisher Books, 1997.
A helpful guide for the early weeks and beyond after the death of a spouse.

Grollman, Earl. *Living When a Loved One Has Died.* Boston: Beacon Press, 1995.

A comforting, inspirational, and insightful book. Rabbi Grollman is an internationally known lecturer, writer, and grief counselor.

Hanson, Warren. *The Next Place.* Minneapolis: Waldman House, 1997.

In picture-book format, The Next Place presents a journey of light, hope, and wonder to a place where earthly hurts are left behind. Suitable for children as well as adults, for persons facing death as well as those grieving.

Hicks, John Mark. *Yet Will I Trust Him: Understanding God in a Suffering World.* Joplin, Mo.: College Press Publishing, 2000.

A reviewer calls this book, "One of the greatest books on human suffering." Out of Hick's own pain at the death of his first wife and the fatal illness of his child, Hicks has written a book in which scriptural and theological thoughts are deep.

Jones, Doris Moreland. *And Not One Bird Stopped Singing: Coping with Transition and Loss in Aging.* Nashville: Upper Room Books, 1997.

A counselor with master's degrees in divinity and sacred theology candidly tells her personal story of the loss of her husband as well as other losses. Her insight and graphic metaphors (such as "spousal death: amputation without anesthesia") are helpful.

Kidd, Sue Monk. *When the Heart Waits: Spiritual Direction for Life's Sacred Questions.* San Francisco: Harper & Row, 1990.

This is a story of a dark season of the soul when the author waited on God. It is a captivating and graceful account of awakening and transformation.

*Kushner, Harold S.. *When Bad Things Happen to Good People.* New York: Schocken Books, 1981.

With deep insight Rabbi Kushner tells the story of his

son's terminal disease and his struggle to understand God. A thought-provoking book for those who ask questions about suffering and for those who are angry with God.

Lambin, Helen Reichert. *The Death of a Husband: Reflections for a Grieving Wife.* Chicago: ACTA Publications, 1998.
Poetry revealing the real feelings that accompany various aspects of grief.

L'Engle, Madeleine. *Two Part Invention: The Story of a Marriage.* New York: Farrar, Straus & Giroux, 1988.
Beloved author L'Engle has written the story of her marriage to actor Hugh Franklin, his death from cancer, her pain related to his dying and death, and the solace she found.

Levang, Elizabeth. *When Men Grieve: Why Men Grieve Differently and How You Can Help Them.* Minneapolis: Fairview Press, 1998.
An insightful book on how men face loss. Because all men are individuals, there are exceptions, but this may lead to better understandings of why we grieve in different ways.

*Lewis, C. S. *A Grief Observed.* Greenwich, Conn.: Seabury Press, 1963.
Well-known author C. S. Lewis's wife died after a short marriage. He candidly shares his grief—never losing sight of God—and comes to some profound and helpful understandings.

Manning, Doug. *Don't Take My Grief Away from Me: How to Walk Through Grief and Learn to Live Again.* Oklahoma City: Insight Press, 1999.
A practical guide for dealing with the emotional and decision-making aspects of grief.

Martin, John D., and Frank D. Ferris. *I Can't Stop Crying; It's So Hard When Someone You Love Dies.* Toronto: Key Porter Books, 1992.
The authors believe that the purpose of grief is to help

reconstruct life after a loss. The key to adjusting to loss is giving oneself permission to feel the pain and emptiness of grief. Three Rs (realize, recognize, and rebuild) are the framework for adjustment.

Moffat, Mary Jane, ed. *In the Midst of Winter: Selections from the Literature of Mourning.* New York: Vintage Books, 1992.
A collection of great writings, including biblical ones, throughout the ages.

*Neufeld, Elsie K. *Dancing in the Dark: A Sister Grieves.* Scottdale, Pa.: Herald Press, 1990.
With informal, yet poetic words, Neufeld tells her story of grief for her brother, who was killed by a drunken driver. Her grieving included dealing with anger at the driver and finding forgiveness.

Noel, Brook, and Pamela D. Blair. *I Wasn't Ready to Say Goodbye: Surviving, Coping, and Healing After the Sudden Death of a Loved One.* Milwaukee: Champion Press, 2000.
In addition to offering an outstanding list of resources, these two who have carefully studied grief offer responses for many of the questions and issues grieving people face.

Nouwen, Henri J. M. *A Letter of Consolation.* San Francisco: Harper & Row, 1982.
In this collection of letters in which Nouwen writes to his father after his mother's death, he reflects on his own loss and makes insightful observations about bereavement after death of a spouse. For those who grieve the death of loved ones and search for transformation.

————. *Can You Drink This Cup?* Notre Dame, Ind.: Ave Maria Press, 1996.
This wise spiritual father explains how the cup of sorrow and the cup of joy are related, helping to put grief into perspective and offering hope to the bereaved.

————. *The Inner Voice of Love: A Journey through Anguish to Freedom.* New York: Doubleday, 1996.

> Nouwen chronicles the most difficult period of his life, a time of intense purification that led to transformation. Written eight years after the fact, these "spiritual imperatives" helped him survive his dark night.

Rolheister, Ronald. *The Holy Longing: The Search for a Christian Spirituality.* New York: Doubleday, 1999.

> Rolheister, a Catholic priest, articulates the longing that is within all humanity, although sometimes not recognized. An easy-to-read theological treatise with practical thoughts about a vivacious spirituality.

Rupp, Joyce. *Praying Our Goodbyes.* Notre Dame, Ind.: Ave Maria Press, 1988.

> A guide to facing endings and nourishing beginnings. Includes the aspects of praying a goodbye: realization, reflection, ritualization, and reorientation.

*Schweibert, Pat, Chuck DeKlyen, and Taylor Bills. *Tear Soup.* Portland, Ore.: Grief Watch, 2001.

> Tear soup is a wonderful picture book for adults written about how we each individually grieve loss in our lives. It offers useful and important information about grief with some new ways to understand and talk about grieving.

Shaw, Luci. *God in the Dark: Through Grief and Beyond.* Grand Rapids, Mich.: Zondervan, 1989.

> Poignant words and poetic lines to tell the story of Shaw's husband's dying and her own grief. At times she had difficulty knowing God, but she honestly faced her doubts.

*Sittser, Gerald. *A Grace Disguised: How the Soul Grows Through Loss.* Grand Rapids, Mich.: Zondervan, 1996.

> An inspirational and profound book about one man's grief work after the death of his wife, daughter, and mother from an auto accident in which he was the driver. Those who read only one book on grief will benefit from choosing this one. Sittser struggles with difficult questions about God.

Smith, Harold Ivan. *A Decembered Grief: Living with Loss While Others are Celebrating*. Kansas City: Beacon Hill, 1999.
>   Stories, quotations, prayers, and suggestions for grieving people during the holidays.

*Weems, Ann. *Psalms of Lament*. Louisville, Ky.: Westminster/ John Knox Press, 1995.
>   These psalms emerge from the depths of the author's grief after the death of her son. A book "for those who are living with scalding tears running down their cheeks," writes the author.

*Wengerd, Sara. *A Healing Grief: Walking with Your Friend Through Loss*. Scottdale, Pa.: Herald Press, 2002.
>   With honesty and tenderness, Wengerd weaves the story of her husband's death and her own grief journey with very practical suggestions for supporting friends who grieve.

Wiebe, Katie Funk. *Alone: A Search for Joy*. Hillsboro, Kan.: Kindred Press, 1987.
>   Written many years after her young husband's death, this is a moving story of his death, her life as a single mother, and her transformation to becoming "no longer a widow."

*Wolfelt, Alan D. *Understanding Your Grief: Ten Essential Touchstones for Finding Hope and Healing Your Heart*. Ft. Collins, Colo.: Companion Press, 2004.
>   The most recent book of many written by the founder and director of the Center for Loss and Life Transition in Fort Collins, Colorado. Wolfelt teaches that it is in mourning that one heals. Grief is a mystery, and mystery can't be understood, but it can be pondered.

———. *Healing a Spouse's Grieving Heart: 100 Practical Ideas After Your Husband or Wife Dies* (Healing a Grieving Heart series). Fort Collins, Colo.: Companion Press, 2003.
>   Wolfelt says that grief is a journey of the soul. He gently presents his ideas on how to mourn (the outward

expression of grief) and on what is thought and felt on the inside of a bereaved person.

*Wolterstorff, Nicholas. *Lament for a Son.* Grand Rapids, Mich.: Eerdmans, 1987.

Personal, emotive, and theological reflections of a father whose son was killed in a mountain climbing accident. In this poetic and profound little book, pertinent for people with all kinds of loss, Wolterstorff struggles with life's difficult questions and points to God.

*Zonnebelt-Smeege, Susan, and Robert DeVries. *Getting to the Other Side of Grief: Overcoming the Loss of a Spouse.* Grand Rapids, Mich.: Baker Books, 1998.

A well-written and easy-to-read book with practical suggestions for processing grief. A nurse/psychologist and a pastor (both widowed and then married to each other) address many of the difficult questions widowed people face. A section of the book discusses new romantic relationships.

*one of my favorite books

Two Additional Resources

Bereavement, a Magazine of Hope and Healing. Bereavement Publishing, 5125 North Union Blvd., Colorado Springs, Colo., 80918. 1-888-604-HOPE. www.bereavementmag.com

Establishing Significance, Understanding Grief, The Gift of Understanding, and *Reconstructing Our Lives* by Doug Manning. Oklahoma City: In-Sight Books, 1999. Special Care Series of four booklets for bereaved people during the first year. P.O. Box 42467, Oklahoma City, OK 73123. 1-800-658-9262.

Notes

Preface

1. Richard Rohr, *Gate of the Temple: Spirituality and Sexuality* (Kansas City, Mo.: National Catholic Reporter Publishing, 1988), Audiocassettes sound recording.

2. Half of all married people will experience the death of a spouse—minus the few couples who die together. Divorce changes the statistic only in that the one who dies is an ex-spouse.

3. In the 1999 U.S. Census, almost half (45 percent) of women over sixty-five were widows. Nearly 700,000 women lose their husbands each year and will be widows for an average of fourteen years. In the same year there were over four times as many widows (8.4 million) as widowers (1.9 million). Cited at http://www.aarp.org/griefandloss/articles/93_a.html (accessed March 1, 2004).

4. Mennonites, the Christian denomination to which I belong, are part of a family of Anabaptists who trace their origins to the Radical Reformation in sixteenth-century Europe. Central to most Anabaptists is church membership based on personal confession of faith, believers baptism, and literal obedience to Jesus' Sermon on the Mount, including nonresistance to violence and war. There are many groups of Mennonites, ranging from theologically conservative to relatively liberal. The Amish are a related group who split from Mennonites in Europe in the late seventeenth century. Most of the Mennonite respondents in my study were from Mennonite Church USA.

5. I arranged for the questionnaires to be returned to me anonymously, being mailed to my advisor at AMBS. I did not see any of the postmarks that might have helped to identify a respondent in a few cases. The returned questionnaire booklets are kept in a locked file. I entered the information into an Excel database that is accessible with my private password. A few people signed their names to their responses, but for the most part I do not know which 152 of the 220 people returned the questionnaires. In an attempt to preserve as much anonymity as possible, I entered the data in a vertical fashion rather than horizontally, that is, I entered the data from pages 1 and 2 from twenty or more respondents before going on to pages 3 and 4. In so doing, any inclination to assume certain answers were coming from a specific individual was minimized. I had randomly assigned names to quotations from anonymous respondents.

Chapter 1

1. Kahlil Gibran, *The Prophet* (New York: Knopf, 1971), 29-30. Gibran (1883–1931) was among the most important Arabic language authors of the early twentieth century. Born in Lebanon, he was a poet, philosopher, and artist. His poetry has been translated into more than twenty languages.

2. Elisabeth Kübler-Ross makes such a statement in *The Wheel of Life: A Memoir of Living and Dying* (New York: Simon and Schuster, 1997), 17. See also Jean Stairs, *Listening for the Soul: Pastoral Care and Spiritual Direction* (Minneapolis: Fortress, 2000), 73-106.

3. Lyn Prashant, "Normalizing the Grief: Degriefing the Body and Mind with Psychosomatic Semantics," in *Massage and Bodywork* (April/May 2002): 86. Prashant is an educator, author, massage therapist, psychotherapist, and certified grief counselor with over twenty years experience in the field. Her training in bereavement counseling and her knowledge of somatic healthcare practices has led her to develop a unique and successful approach to grief counseling called "degriefing." The Degriefing Process is a holistic approach to healing grief-related pain. For more information, see www.degriefing.com.

4. Judith Viorst, *Necessary Losses: The Loves, Illusions, Dependencies and Impossible Expectations That All of Us Have to Give Up in Order to Grow* (New York: Fawcett, 1986), 366-8.

5. Sherill Hostetter, "Embracing Pain: Looking to God in the Midst of Loss," in *Soul Care: How to Plan and Guide Inspirational Retreats*, ed. Rose Mary Stutzman (Scottdale, Pa.: Herald Press, 2003), 109.

6. Joan D. Chittister, *Scarred by Struggle, Transformed by Hope* (Grand Rapids, Mich.: Eerdmans, 2003), 19.

7. Ibid., 64.

8. Gale Livengood, of Middlebury, Indiana, and her late husband, Ken, were in a tornado in Kansas that destroyed their home. Ken was killed in a motorcycle accident in 2003.

9. Viktor E. Frankl, *Man's Search for Meaning* (Boston: Beacon Press, 1963), 55.

10. Elsie Neufeld, *Dancing in the Dark: A Sister Grieves* (Scottdale, Pa.: Herald Press, 1990), 13.

11. Wayne E. Oates, *Grief, Transition, and Loss: A Pastor's Practical Guide* (Minneapolis: Fortress Press, 1997), 39.

12. Doug Manning, *Establishing Significance* (Oklahoma City: In-Sight Books, 1993), 11.

13. Oates, 39.

14. Peg Elliott Mayo and David Feinstein, *Rituals for Living and Dying: How We Can Turn Loss and the Fear of Death into an Affirmation of Life* (HarperSanFrancisco, 1990), 124. Mayo is a psychotherapist whose husband and young-adult son died by suicide.

15. James E. Loder, *The Logic of the Spirit: Human Development in Theological Perspective* (San Francisco: Jossey-Bass, 1998), 278.

16. C. S. Lewis, *A Grief Observed* (Greenwich, Conn.: Seabury Press, 1963), 65.

17. Ibid., 70.

18. Doris Moreland Jones, *And Not One Bird Stopped Singing: Coping with Transition and Loss in Aging* (Nashville: Upper Room Books, 1997), 15.

19. Lyn Prashant, *The New Art of Degriefing: Transforming Grief Using Body/Mind Therapies* (San Anselmo, Calif.: Prashant, 2002), xix.

20. In the social sciences, the word *gender* has come to refer to social constructs of male and female, whereas *sex* refers to biological characteristics of male and female. In this book and particularly in the questionnaire, the words *gender* and *sex* are used interchangeably.

21. Eugene Peterson, *Five Smooth Stones for Pastoral Work* (Grand Rapids, Mich.: Eerdmans, 1980), 146.

22. Henri J. M. Nouwen, *The Wounded Healer* (New York: Doubleday, 1972), 60.

23. This question was asked about the first months after the death. A later question asking about the overall major task of grief elicited many more statements about identity.

24. Frankl, 76.

25. Quoted in Henri J. M. Nouwen, *The Genesee Diary: Report from a Trappist Monastery* (Garden City, N.Y.: Image Books, 1981), 121-2.

26. Don Postema, *Space for God: The Study and Practice of Prayer and Spirituality* (Grand Rapids, Mich.: Board of Publications of the Christian Reformed Church, 1983), 135.

27. Charles Wesley, *Hymns and Sacred Poems*, 1742, as cited in *Hymnal Accompaniment Handbook*, eds. Kenneth Nafziger and Rebecca Slough (Elgin, Ill.: Brethren Press; Newton, Kan.: Faith & Life Press; Scottdale, Pa.: Mennonite Publishing House, 1993), 321.

28. Elie Wiesel, *The Gates of the Forest* (New York: Schocken Books, 1982), 180.

29. Ronald Rolheiser offers "A Spirituality of the Paschal Mystery," in *The Holy Longing: The Search for a Christian Spirituality* (New York: Doubleday, 1999), 141-66. Jean Stairs addresses the mystery in "The Soul's Rhythm: Death and Resurrection," in *Listening for the Soul Pastoral Care and Spiritual Direction* (Minneapolis: Fortress, 2000), 73-106.

30. Stairs, 86.

31. Karl Barth, *Church Dogmatics*, 4:2, 487, and *Predigten*, 230, quoted in Kathleen D. Billman and Daniel L. Migliore, *Rachel's Cry: Prayer of Lament and Rebirth of Hope* (Cleveland: United Church Press, 1999), 64. Barth (1886-1968) is considered by some to be the greatest Protestant theologian of the twentieth century and possibly the greatest since the Reformation.

32. Jürgen Moltmann, *The Crucified God: The Cross of Christ as the Foundation and Criticism of Christian Theology*, 153, and *The Way of Jesus Christ: Christology in Messianic Dimensions*, 152, as cited in Billman and Migliore, 68. Moltmann, professor emeritus from Tübingen University, is one of the world's leading Protestant theologians. He is author of *Theology of Hope*; the theme that runs throughout his writings is hope.

33. Dietrich Bonhoeffer, *Letters and Papers from Prison* (London: Collins, 1959), 122. Bonhoeffer (1906-1945), an outstanding

German theologian, a brilliant thinker and writer, a compelling poet, and a beloved pastor, was imprisoned and killed by the Nazis.

34. Harold S. Kushner, *When Bad Things Happen to Good People* (New York: Schocken Books, 1981), 6.

35. Willard M. Swartley, "The Pastor as Healer," in *The Heart of the Matter: Pastoral Ministry in Anabaptist Perspective*, ed. Erick Sawatzky (Telford, Pa.: Cascadia, 2004), 156-7.

36. Gerald Sittser, A *Grace Disguised: How the Soul Grows Through Loss* (Grand Rapids, Mich.: Zondervan, 1996). Sittser is professor of religion and philosophy at Whitworth College, Spokane, Washington.

37. Nicholas Wolterstorff, *Lament for a Son* (Grand Rapids, Mich.: Eerdmans, 1987). Wolterstorff is professor emeritus of philosophical theology at Yale University Divinity School.

38. Kushner, 148. He also says, "The ability to forgive and the ability to love are the weapons God has given us to enable us to live fully."

39. Sittser, 115.

40. Ibid., 151.

41. Dorothee Soelle, *Suffering* (Philadelphia: Fortress Press, 1975), 2-3.

42. Myrna Miller, "The Omnipotence of God: Trusting in God's Love" (senior integration paper, Associated Mennonite Biblical Seminary, 2004), 16.

43. Wolterstorff, 81.

44. Henri J. M. Nouwen, *Can You Drink the Cup?* (Notre Dame, Ind.: Ave Maria Press, 1996), 38.

45. Ibid., 46-7.

46. Gibran, 29.

47. Marlene Kropf and Eddy Hall, *Praying with the Anabaptists: The Secret of Bearing Fruit* (Newton, Kan.: Faith & Life Press, 1994), 105.

48. Bonhoeffer, 171-72.

49. Mennonite minister Eugene Herr was cofounder and long-time codirector of The Hermitage, a retreat center in Michigan.

50. Kahlil Gibran, *A Tear and a Smile*, trans. H. M. Nahmad (New York: Knopf, 1950), xxi.

51. Henri J. M. Nouwen, *A Letter of Consolation* (San Francisco: Harper & Row, 1982), 42, 43.

52. Wolterstorff, 49.

53. Nouwen, *Wounded Healer*, 66.

54. Frankl, 87-8.

55. Chittister, xi.

56. Chittister, 75-6.

57. Cited in Chittister, 80.

58. Prashant, xviii.

59. Peterson, 132.

Chapter 2

1. AMBS Professor Emeritus Perry Yoder describes this verse as the heart of the Psalter.

2. Alan D. Wolfelt, *The Journey Through Grief: Reflections on Healing* (Ft. Collins, Colo.: Companion Press, 2003), 53.

3. Joan D. Chittister, *Scarred by Struggle, Transformed by Hope* (Grand Rapids, Mich.: Eerdmans, 2003), 23.

4. Ronald Rolheiser, *The Holy Longing: The Search for a Christian Spirituality* (New York: Doubleday, 1999), 163.

5. Alan D. Wolfelt, *Understanding Your Grief: Ten Essential Touchstones for Finding Hope and Healing Your Heart* (Ft. Collins, Colo.: Companion Press, 2004), 22.

6. Since many people use the terms interchangeably, I do not strictly follow Wolfelt's definitions.

7. Walter Brueggemann, *The Message of the Psalms: A Theological Commentary* (Minneapolis: Augsburg, 1984), 20.

8. Quoted in Kathleen D. Billman and Daniel L. Migliore, *Rachel's Cry: Prayer of Lament and Rebirth of Hope* (Cleveland: United Church Press, 1999), 62.

9. Billman and Migliore, 7.

10. Ibid., 24.

11. Brueggemann as quoted in Donald Capps, *Biblical Approaches to Pastoral Counseling* (Philadelphia: Westminster Press, 1981), 74.

12. Ibid., 75.

13. Billman and Migliore suggest that there may be a "correlation between the lack of corporate lament in the Christian church and increased susceptibility to amnesia and nostalgia," 92.

14. Viktor E. Frankl, *Man's Search for Meaning* (Boston: Beacon Press, 1963), 74.

15. Walter Brueggemann, "Foreword," in Ann Weems, *Psalms of Lament* (Louisville: Westminster/John Knox Press, 1995), x.

16. Ibid., xi.

17. J. David Pleins, *The Psalms: Songs of Tragedy, Hope and Justice* (Maryknoll, N.Y.: Orbis, 1993), 14.

18. Weems, xi.

19. Pleins, 15.

20. Brueggemann as cited in Weems, xi.

21. Billman and Migliore, 29.

22. C. S. Lewis, *A Grief Observed* (San Francisco: Harper & Row, 1961), 18.

23. Ibid., 19.

24. Ibid., 10.

25. Brueggemann as cited in Weems, xiii.

26. North American hospital personnel referred to this kind of episode as an "attack-ie."

27. Months after my father's death, a wise counselor helped me to lament. Singing "Until Then" was not enough for me. When my husband died later, I expressed my grief forthrightly.

28. Chittister, 40.

29. Sue Monk Kidd, *When the Heart Waits* (San Francisco: Harper & Row, 1990). Kidd describes a difficult time in her life as a metamorphosis from caterpillar to butterfly.

30. Elmer A. Martens, *Jeremiah: Believers Church Bible Commentary* (Scottdale, Pa.: Herald Press, 1986), 193.

31. R. E. Clements, *Jeremiah, Interpretation: A Bible Commentary for Teaching and Preaching* (Atlanta: John Knox Press, 1988), 188.

32. Gordon Dyck is an ordained minister in the Mennonite Church who worked for many years as a psychotherapist at Oaklawn, a mental health facility in Elkhart County, Indiana.

33. Lewis, 65.

34. Carla's great response is the title of a book: Linda Feinberg, *I'm Grieving as Fast as I Can: How Young Widows and Widowers Can Cope and Heal* (Far Hills, N.J.: New Horizon Press, 1994).

35. Fifty-one of the respondents had remarried, so this question was answered by 90 percent of those for whom this question pertained.

36. Susan Zonnebelt-Smeege and Robert DeVries, *Getting to the Other Side of Grief: Overcoming the Loss of a Spouse* (Grand Rapids, Mich.: Baker Books, 1998), 64.

37. Elisabeth Kübler-Ross, *The Wheel of Life: A Memoir of Living and Dying* (New York: Simon and Schuster, 1997), Audiocassettes sound recording.

38. Steven Moss, "The Grief-Work Cycle in Judaism," in *Death and Ministry: Pastoral Care of the Dying and the Bereaved,* ed. J. Donald Bane et. al. (New York: Seabury Press, 1975), 109-10.

39. Ibid., 110.

40. Joyce Rupp, *Praying Our Goodbyes* (Notre Dame, Ind.: Ave Maria Press, 1988), 78-89.

41. Ibid., 87.

42. Sidney Zisook, ed., *Biopsychosocial Aspects of Bereavement* (Washington, D.C.: American Psychiatric Press, 1987), 24-5.

43. J. William Worden, *Grief Counseling and Grief Therapy: A Handbook for the Mental Health Practitioner*, 3d ed. (New York: Springer, 2002).

44. J. William Worden, http://www.aarp.org/griefandloss/articles/12_a.html (accessed March 14, 2004.)

45. Joan Didion, *The Year of Magical Thinking* (New York: Knopf, 2005).

46. Wolfelt, *Journey Through Grief*, 53.

47. Dennis Klass, Phyllis R. Silverman, and Steven L. Nickman, *Continuing Bonds: New Understandings of Grief* (Bristol, Pa.: Taylor and Francis, 1996), 148.

48. Helena Znaniecka Lopata, "Widowhood and Husband Sanctification" in *Continuing Bonds: New Understandings of Grief*, ed. Dennis Klass, Phyllis R. Silverman, and Steven L. Nickman (Bristol, Pa.: Taylor and Francis, 1996), 150-1.

49. Frankl, 86-9.

Chapter 3

1. Quoted in Joan D. Chittister, *Scarred by Struggle, Transformed by Hope* (Grand Rapids, Mich.: Eerdmans, 2003), 77.

2. Urban T. Holmes III, *Spirituality for Ministry* (San Francisco: Harper & Row, 1982).

3. Unpublished poem. Yoder Miller is a spiritual director and retreat leader from Goshen, Indiana.

4. Chittister, 1.

5. Kathleen Norris, *The Cloister Walk* (New York: Riverhead, 1996), 252.

6. Chittister, 68.

7. Jean Stairs, *Listening for the Soul: Pastoral Care and Spiritual Direction* (Minneapolis: Fortress, 2000), 90, 206.

8. Ibid., 81, 88.

9. Ibid., 88.

10. Ibid., 89, 92.

11. Ibid., 89.

12. Quoted by Joyce Rupp on web site describing her audio book *The Liberated Heart*, 2003, http://www.joycerupp.com/tapes.html#heart (accessed August 2, 2004).

13. Joyce Rupp, *The Liberated Heart.*

14. I understand "finding one's true self" to mean becoming more human in the light of God, becoming closer to what we interpret to be God's intention for humanity.

15. H. Tristram Engelhardt Jr., "The Concept of Bereavement," in *Death and Ministry: Pastoral Care of the Dying and the Bereaved*, ed. J. Donald Bane et al. (New York: Seabury Press, 1975), 220.

16. Todd F. Davis and Kenneth Womack, "Reading the Ethics of Mourning in the Poetry of Donald Hall," in *Response to Death: Literary Work on Mourning*, ed. Christian Riegel (Edmonton: University of Alberta, 2005),178.

17. Karl Rahner, (1904-1984), was a German Jesuit priest who is widely considered to have been one of the foremost Roman Catholic theologians of the twentieth century.

18. Annice Callahan, *Traditions of Spiritual Guidance*, 341, as quoted in *People's Companion to the Breviary: The Liturgy of the Hours with Inclusive Language, vol. 1* (Indianapolis: Carmelites of Indianapolis, 1997), 119.

19. Quoted in J. Philip Newell, *Listening to the Heartbeat of God: A Celtic Spirituality* (New York: Paulist Press, 1997), 79. George MacLeod was the founder of the Iona Community, a spiritual community on the island of Iona in western Scotland.

20. Judith Viorst, *Necessary Losses: The Loves, Illusions, Dependencies and Impossible Expectations That All of Us Have to Give Up in Order to Grow* (New York: Fawcett, 1986), 25.

21. James E. Loder, *The Logic of the Spirit: Human Development in Theological Perspective* (San Francisco: Jossey-Bass, 1998), 10-12.

22. Sheila Fabricant Linn, William Emerson, Dennis Linn, and Matthew Linn, *Remembering Our Home: Healing Hurts and Receiving Gifts from Conception to Birth* (New York: Paulist Press, 1999), 14-15. The Linns associate with a Jesuit Community in Minnesota and work as a team integrating physical, emotional, and spiritual wholeness in retreat settings and as authors of many books. Emerson joined them as a coauthor of this book.

23. Richard Rohr, *Gate of the Temple: Spirituality and Sexuality* (Kansas City, Mo.: National Catholic Reporter Publishing, 1988), Audiocassettes sound recording.

24. Loder, 150.

25. Ibid., 149.

26. Ibid., 170.

27. Ibid.

28. Chittister, 39.

29. Tamara Ferguson, "How Young Widows have Coped with their Problems," in *Perspectives on Bereavement,* ed. Irwin Gerber et. al. (New York: Arno Press, 1979), 33-46.

30. Jacqueline Syrup Bergan and S. Marie Schwan, *Surrender: A Guide to Prayer* (Winona, Minn.: Saint Mary's Press, 1986), 59.

31. Erich Fromm, *The Art of Loving,* as quoted in Mary Rosera Joyce and Robert E. Joyce, *New Dynamics in Sexual Love: A Revolutionary Approach to Marriage and Celibacy* (Collegeville, Minn.: St. John's University Press, 1970), 51.

32. Harold never did "drag me around." When he went to events in which he had more interest than I, he would invite me to go along. Sometimes I did, but not always. I had a choice.

33. Robert F. Morneau, *Mantras from a Poet: Jessica Powers,* 58-9, as cited in *People's Companion to the Breviary,* 255.

34. Ronald Rolheiser, *The Holy Longing: The Search for a Christian Spirituality* (New York: Doubleday, 1999), 208.

35. Loder, 286.

36. Sidney Zisook and Stephen R. Shuchter, "A Multidimensional Model of Spousal Bereavement," in *Biopsychosocial Aspects of Bereavement,* ed. Sidney Zisook (Washington, D.C.: American Psychiatric Press, 1987), 46.

37. Sidney Zisook, Stephen R. Shuchter, and Lucy E. Lyons, "Adjustment to Widowhood," in *Biopsychosocial Aspects of Bereavement,* ed. Sidney Zisook (Washington, D.C.: American Psychiatric Press, 1987), 52.

38. Ibid., 62-5.

39. Chittister, 35.

40. Katie Funk Wiebe, *Alone: A Search for Joy* (Hillsboro, Kan.: Kindred Press, 1987), 9.

41. Loder, 222.

42. Ibid., 248.

Chapter 4

1. John S. Dunne, *The Reasons of the Heart,* as quoted in *A Guide to Prayer for Ministers and Other Servants,* ed. Rueben P. Job and Norman Shawchuck, (Nashville, Tenn.: Upper Room, 1983), 176.

2. Peter McWilliams, 1970, in David M. Schnarch, *Constructing the Sexual Crucible: An Integration of Sexual and Marital Therapy* (New York: Norton, 1991), vi.

3. C. S. Lewis, *A Grief Observed* (Greenwich, Conn.: Seabury Press, 1963), 67.

4. Richard Rohr, *Gate of the Temple: Spirituality and Sexuality* (Kansas City, Mo.: National Catholic Reporter Publishing, 1988). Audiocassettes sound recording.

5. This comment is not intended to negate the reality or value of life for people who intentionally live as hermits. People who live successfully as hermits seem to have a relationship with God that apparently compensates for regular human contact. However, according to Rohr, people are not ready for a life of solitude until they have learned to live well in community.

6. Willard Krabill, "The Gift and Intimacy," in *Sexuality: God's Gift*, ed. Anne Krabill Hershberger (Scottdale, Pa.: Herald Press, 1999), 49.

7. More information about important support is given in chapter 5.

8. Two people said no "couple friends" stood by them. One of these was a woman over eighty who said that all her former friends had died. The other was a woman in her sixties who said that singles are treated like fifth wheels.

9. Comparing this identified interest to other groups of single people, I conclude the following: (1) The idea of widowers missing female friendship was seldom mentioned in responses to my questionnaire or in other sources of information. This does not necessarily mean that it is less common, as only half as many men as women responded to the questionnaire, and men tend to talk less about their feelings. Also, men may have hesitated to reveal this to a female researcher. In addition, it is socially acceptable for men to take initiative in male-female relationships, and although female initiative is more acceptable than in the past, many women do not feel free to take initiative, particularly women of older generations. (2) Although I have not made a serious study of divorced women, my casual observation is that missing male friendship is not as big an issue for them. I wonder if this is because many divorced women do continue to relate to a man—their former husband—and that relationship is often less than pleasant.

10. Rohr, *Gate of the Temple.*

11. Richard J. Foster, *The Challenge of the Disciplined Life: Christian Reflections on Money, Sex and Power* (San Francisco: Harper & Row, 1985), 91.

12. Foster, 92. There is not agreement that Karl Barth is the first major theologian to illuminate this concept. Philip Newell says that the British/Celtic theologian Pelagius clearly established this in the in the late fourth and early fifth centuries.

13. Ibid., 92.

14. Although *relationship* can have broad meanings, I use it in this part of the book, as I did in the questionnaire, to refer to a romantic involvement.

15. While thirty-seven women and three men left this question blank, it is not assumed that these people did not feel any attractions. They may have simply preferred not to reveal this information.

16. Susan Zonnebelt-Smeege and Robert DeVries, *Getting to the Other Side of Grief: Overcoming the Loss of a Spouse* (Grand Rapids, Mich.: Baker Books, 1998), 197. Two people who responded to the Living Well questionnaire were widowed, remarried, and then divorced.

Although this seems to be a low percentage, the questionnaire did not specifically ask when marriages occurred in relation to spousal death, so the percentages of respondents who married within two years and then divorced is not available.

17. The questionnaire asked if people dated/courted/spent time with a person of the other gender, recognizing that terms used for male-female friendships and activities vary. For the purposes of simplicity, the term *dating* will be used in reporting the information. At the same time it is recognized that some respondents spent time with a person of the opposite sex with no intention to marry and perhaps without a romantic component.

18. Elizabeth Levang, *When Men Grieve: Why Men Grieve Differently and How You Can Help Them* (Minneapolis: Fairview Press, 1998).

19. However, the pattern of later dating for women may be a factor in the differences in timing noted, in that women who participated in the study and had not dated when completing the questionnaire may begin dating relationships in the future.

20. This column does not equal 100 percent because three women did not specify the time at which new attractions were first experienced.

21. Given these statistics, a high percentage of men responded to my questionnaire: 69 percent are women and 30 percent are men. (Note: 1 percent did not indicate gender.)

22. Peter McWilliams, in Schnarch, vi.

23. The percentages in these columns are the numbers who remarried in relation to the numbers of people who fit the category at the time of the survey, not the total number of people widowed.

24. One man did not indicate when he was widowed, so although he is included in the totals, he is not in the columns headed "total" and "men," and the numbers in the column do not add up to the total.

25. Miriam S. Moss and Sidney Z. Moss, "Remarriage of Widowed Persons: A Triadic Relationship," in *Continuing Bonds: New Understandings of Grief*, eds. Dennis Klass, Phyllis R. Silverman, and Steven L. Nickman (Bristol, Pa.: Taylor and Francis, 1996), 163-78.

26. Ibid., 176,

27. Helena Znaniecka Lopata, "Widowhood and Husband Sanctification," in *Continuing Bonds: New Understandings of Grief*, eds. Dennis Klass, Phyllis R. Silverman, and Steven L. Nickman (Bristol, Pa.: Taylor and Francis, 1996), 152.

28. A woman who was married for the first time to a man who had been widowed noted that it was refreshing to finally find some books written "especially for me!" Three of these are *Second Wife: Stories and Wisdom from Women Who Have Married Widowers* by Martha Denlinger Stahl (Intercourse, Pa.: Good Books, 2005), *Past: Perfect! Present: Tense! Insights from One Woman's Journey As the Wife of a Widower* by Julie Donner Anderson (Lincoln, Neb.: iUniverse, 2003), and *Second Wives: The Pitfalls and Rewards of Marrying Widowers and Divorced Men* by Susan Shapiro Barash (Far Hills, N.J.: New Horizon, 2000).

29. Ronald Rolheiser, *The Holy Longing: The Search for a Christian Spirituality* (New York: Doubleday, 1999), 192.

30. Ibid., 194.

31. Ibid., 198.

32. Foster, 99.

33. Donald Goergen, *The Sexual Celibate* (Garden City, N.Y.: Seabury Press, 1975), 34.

34. Mary Rosera Joyce and Robert E. Joyce, *New Dynamics in Sexual Love: A Revolutionary Approach to Marriage and Celibacy* (Collegeville, Minn.: St. John's University Press, 1970), 56.

35. Keith Clark, *Being Sexual . . . and Celibate* (Notre Dame, Ind.: Ave Maria Press, 1986), 19.

36. James B. Nelson, *Body Theology* (Louisville: Westminster/John Knox, 1992), 45.

37. For a summary of Erikson's theory, see his final work, *The Life Cycle Completed* (New York: Norton, 1982).

38. Anne Krabill Hershberger and Willard Krabill, "The Gift," in *Sexuality: God's Gift*, ed. Anne Krabill Hershberger (Scottdale, Pa.: Herald Press, 1999), 21, 31.

39. This person did not indicate his or her gender.

40. People were also asked if what they missed most about the deceased spouse changed as time went on. Fifty-seven respondents said yes, but changes identified seem unremarkable. Four people indicated that sexual interest increased. Some indicated that the pain of the absence continued. Most indicated they were beginning to make adjustments for the absence.

41. Rohr, *Gate of the Temple*.

42. James E. Loder, *The Logic of the Spirit: Human Development in Theological Perspective* (San Francisco: Jossey-Bass, 1998), 223.

43. Goergen, 61.

44. Loder, 150.

45. Henry Staten, *Eros in Mourning: Homer to Lacan* (Baltimore: Johns Hopkins University Press, 2002), xi.

46. Yorifumi Yaguchi, "Praying Mantis" in *Three Mennonite Poets* (Intercourse, Pa.: Good Books, 1986), 46.)

47. Elizabeth Clark, ed., *St. Augustine on Marriage and Sexuality* (Washington, D.C.: Catholic University of America Press, 1996), 48.

48. J. Philip Newell, *Listening for the Heartbeat of God: A Celtic Spirituality* (New York: Paulist Press, 1997), 13-14.

49. Ibid, 14.

50. Ibid.

51. Augustine, *The City of God*, as quoted in Goergen, 36-7.

52. Goergen, 56-8.

53. Ibid., 58-9.

54. Henri J. M. Nouwen, *Clowning in Rome: Reflections on Solitude, Celibacy, Prayer, and Contemplation* (Garden City, N.Y.: Image, 1979), 45.

55. Henri J. M. Nouwen, "Celibacy and the Holy," in *Celibate Loving: Encounter in Three Dimensions*, ed. Mary Anne Huddleston (Ramsey, N.J.: Paulist Press, 1984), 164-5.

56. Joyce and Joyce, 52.

57. Ibid.

58. *Relationships* will now be used in its broader meaning of connectedness and friendships.

59. Richard Rohr, "To Unveil Our Faces: Reflections on Marriage and Celibacy," *Sojourners* 8 (May 1979): 22.

60. Kathleen D. Billman and Daniel L. Migliore, *Rachel's Cry: Prayer of Lament and Rebirth of Hope* (Cleveland: United Church Press, 1999), 80. While Freud's views continue to influence clinical perspectives on grief, they are sharply criticized by some leading theorists.

61. Kathleen Norris, *The Cloister Walk* (New York: Riverhead, 1996), 254.

62. Mary Rosera Joyce, *How Can a Man and Woman be Friends?* (Collegeville, Minn.: The Liturgical Press, 1977), 27. In a few pages Joyce carefully and logically explains a healthy way to respond to sexual impulses. In my thirty-five years of study, reflection, and teaching on areas related to human sexuality, I have not found a better description of a healthy and morally-sound way to hold sexual energy. In addition, Willard Krabill, Goshen College campus physician emeritus, has found that in his decades of practicing medicine and studying and teaching human sexuality, this succinct booklet is one of the best resources available for promoting healthy celibate living.

63. Ibid., 29.

64. Ibid., 31-3.

65. Ibid., 37-8.

66. Ibid., 39.

67. Ibid., 39-40.

68. Ibid., 41.

69. Ibid., 42.

70. Ibid., 44.

71. Ibid., 45.

72. Goergen, 61. Goergen explains self-actualization in a section entitled "Maslow, Sexuality and Self-Actualization," citing: Abraham Maslow, *Motivation and Personality: Religion, Values, and Peak Experiences* (New York: Harper & Row, 1970), 187-8.

73. Ibid., 62.

74. Ibid., 61-2.

75. Rolheiser, 194, 193.

76. Ibid., 204-11.

77. Gabrielle Brown, *The New Celibacy: Why More Men and Women are Abstaining from Sex—and Enjoying It More* (New York: McGraw Hill, 1980), 28.

78. Brown reports on couples "who have found that being celibate from time to time—even for a long period of time—provides certain profound benefits to help sustain growth and love in marriage. Some decide to be celibate to achieve the benefits of a fuller love; others become celibate and then realize the benefits they have been experiencing through the growth of love. In either situation it is the expansion of love which is desired and created" (143). Brown also includes a married woman's

report on periods of celibacy within marriage: "Celibacy kind of lets us be spiritual together. When we have sex again, we don't want it to be a downer but an act of worship. We see sex as being transformed into a different kind of experience through celibacy—making our love stronger within each of us and then into each other" (149). These illuminate a broader value of celibacy; however, celibacy within marriage was not a concern of my project.

79. Ibid., 114.

80. This section is longer than some other sections intentionally, partly because of the scarcity of recent literature about masturbation or self-pleasuring from a Christian perspective and also because it is a topic of interest to many widowed people.

81. The story of Onan in Genesis 38:6-10 has sometimes been mistaken for a commentary on masturbation. It is rather a story of *coitus interruptus* and has to do with refusing to follow cultural expectation. It has also been suggested that myrrh in Song of Solomon 5:5 refers to semen resulting from masturbation: "I arose to open to my beloved; and my hands dripped with myrrh, my fingers with liquid myrrh, upon the handles of the bolt."

82. Stephen Greenblatt, "Me, Myself, and I," *The New York Review of Books* 51, no. 6 (April 8, 2004): 32.

83. Thomas W. Laqueur, *Solitary Sex: A Cultural History of Masturbation* (New York: Zone, 2003), 13-14. *Onania* had an extremely long and descriptive subtitle: *The Heinous Sin of Self Pollution, and all its Frightful Consequences, in both SEXES Considered, with Spiritual and Physical Advice to those who have already injured themselves by the abominable practice. And seasonal Admonition to the Youth of the nation of Both SEXES . . .*

84. Ibid., 30.

85. Ibid., 278.

86. Ibid., 292.

87. Gary Kelly, *Sexuality Today* (New York: McGraw Hill, 2001), 351.

88. Adrian Thatcher, *Liberating Sex: A Christian Sexual Theology* (London: SPCK, 1993), 181.

89. Ibid., 183-4.

90. United Presbyterian Church USA General Assembly, *Sexuality and the Human Community* (Philadelphia: Office of the General Assembly, 1970), 14-15.

91. Presbyterian Church USA and Reformed Church in America, *God's Gift of Sexuality* (Louisville, Ky.: Presbyterian Publishing House, 1989) 12-13.

92. J. Lorne Peachey, ed., "What about Masturbation?" *With*, July 1972, 25-9.

93. J. Lorne Peachey and Everett J. Thomas, *What Really Matters: Conversation Starters for Men* (Newton, Kan.: Faith & Life, 2002), 32.

94. J. Howard Kauffman and Leo Driedger, *The Mennonite Mosaic: Identity and Modernization* (Scottdale, Pa.: Herald Press, 1991), 192.

95. *Human Sexuality in the Christian Life: A Working Document for Study and Dialogue* (Newton, Kan.: Faith & Life Press; Scottdale,

Pa.: Herald Press, 1985), 121-2. Part of this excerpt is quoted from Goergen, *The Sexual Celibate.*

96. Evelyn Eaton Whitehead and James D. Whitehead, *Wisdom of the Body: Making Sense of Our Sexuality* (New York: Crossroads, 2001), 154-66 passim.

97. William R. Stayton, "A Theology of Sexual Pleasure," in *Christian Perspectives on Sexuality and Gender*, ed. Adrian Thatcher and Elizabeth Stuart (Grand Rapids, Mich.: Eerdmans, 1996), 340.

98. Zonnebelt-Smeege and DeVries, 97.

99. Joyce Brothers, *Widowed* (New York: Simon and Schuster, 1990), 201.

100. Although there are various definitions of celibacy, I am using the term to refer to a state of not engaging in genital intercourse. A person can be celibate for a period of time or for a lifetime.

101. Humans are created as sexual beings and we relate to others out of our sexuality. In the broad sense of the word, we are sexually active in all our relationships. However, in this treatise I am using "sexually active" in a more narrow sense, referring specifically to sexual intercourse.

102. Stephen R. Shuchter, *Dimensions of Grief: Adjusting to the Death of a Spouse* (San Francisco: Jossey-Bass, 1986), 111.

103. Respondents were asked to check as many as applied from a list including "other."

104. These figures are below those estimated from several surveys in the United States, particularly for males. One source of information is June M. Reinisch and Ruth Beasley, *The Kinsey Institute New Report on Sex: What You Must Know to be Sexually Literate* (New York: Martin Press, 1990), 95, which states, "Among the thousands of people interviewed by Kinsey during the 1940s and 1950s, 94 percent of males and 40 percent of females reported having masturbated to orgasm. More recent studies report that about the same number of males masturbate but that the percentage of females has increased to around 70 percent (or more, depending on the study)."

105. Carlfred B. Broderick and Jessie Bernard, eds., *The Individual, Sex and Society: A Siecus Handbook for Teachers and Counselors* (Baltimore: Johns Hopkins Press, 1969), 325.

106. Whitehead and Whitehead, 162.

107. Foster identifies three moral questions regarding masturbation: the connection with sexual fantasies, the tendency of masturbation to become obsessive, and the depersonalization of masturbation—that which does not lead to a deep personal relationship with another (125).

108. Ibid., 127.

109. Douglas E. P. Rosenau, "Sexuality and the Single Person," in *Christian Perspectives on Sexuality and Gender*, ed. Adrian Thatcher and Elizabeth Stuart (Grand Rapids, Mich.: Eerdmans, 1996), 421.

110. Joseph Kotva, e-mail and interview by author at AMBS, September 20, 2004.

111. Thatcher, 185. A valid concern about masturbation is that it can be associated with pornography. Thatcher calls pornography "the unac-

ceptable face of lust" (187). Materials that treat women as sex objects or contribute to misogynistic attitudes are clearly unacceptable. Using pornographic materials for sexual arousal that then leads to masturbation is a distorted use of sexuality, and masturbation or any sexual behavior in this connection is objectionable.

112. Brothers, 202. I wondered if there was some research on which Brothers based her statement, but I was unable to find a published report of such research and did not get a response to my inquiry of her.

113. And one of unknown gender.

114. John E. Perito, *Contemporary Catholic Sexuality: What is Taught and What is Practiced* (New York: Crossroad, 2003), 91.

115. Rolheiser, 221.

Chapter 5

1. Quoted in Wayne E. Oates, *The Presence of God in Pastoral Counseling* (Waco, Tex.: Word Books, 1986), 116.

2. Todd F. Davis and Kenneth Womack, "Reading the Ethics of Mourning in the Poetry of Donald Hall," in *Response to Death: Literary Work on Mourning*, ed. Christian Riegel (Edmonton: University of Alberta, 2005), 161-76.

3. Christie Cozad Neuger, *Counseling Women: A Narrative, Pastoral Approach* (Minneapolis: Augsburg-Fortress, 2001), x.

4. Ibid., x.

5. Ibid., 44.

6. Ibid., 141-7.

7. Joyce Rupp, *Praying Our Goodbyes* (Notre Dame, Ind.: Ave Maria Press, 1988), chap. 2.

8. This phrase is taken from the title of an excellent book by Daniel S. Schipani, *The Way of Wisdom in Pastoral Counseling* (Elkhart, Ind.: Institute of Mennonite Studies, 2003).

9. Schipani, *The Way of Wisdom*, 114-15.

10. Daniel S. Schipani, "The Pastor as Caregiving Sage," in *The Heart of the Matter: Pastoral Ministry in Anabaptist Perspective*, ed. Erick Sawatzky (Telford, Pa.: Cascadia, 2004), 198-9.

11. Ibid., 198, 199.

12. Henri J. M. Nouwen, *The Wounded Healer* (New York: Doubleday, 1972), back cover.

13. Ibid., 88.

14. Margaret G. Alter, *Resurrection Psychology: An Understanding of Human Personality Based on the Life and Teachings of Jesus* (Chicago: Loyola University Press, 1994), 165.

15. James E. Miller, "If I Am Not for Myself: Caring for Yourself as a Caregiver for Those Who Grieve," in *Living with Grief: At Work, at School, at Worship*, eds. Joyce D. Davidson and Kenneth J. Doka, Hospice Foundation of America (Levittown, Pa.: Brunner/Mazel, 1999), 213.

16. Ibid., 214-22.

17. Nouwen, 38.

18. David H. Tripp is an AMBS adjunct faculty member.

19. Gayle Gerber Koontz, "After a Death: Theology and Christian Funeral Practices," *Vision: A Journal for Church and Theology* 5, no. 1 (Spring 2004): 12-19 passim.

20. Wolfelt made this comment in a seminar held in Ft. Wayne, Indiana, on April 15, 2004.

21. Alter, 95.

22. Ibid., 105, 109.

23. Ibid., 110, 112, 115.

24. Edie Devers, *Goodbye Again: Experiences with Departed Loved Ones* (Kansas City: Andrews and McMeel, 1997). After-death "communication" is an instance of a living person experiencing some form of personal contact with someone who has died, most often someone the living was very close to. It often has a profound effect on the survivor.

25. Communication is a two-way process that, strictly speaking, cannot happen with a person who has died. However, "communication" or "receiving messages" can take place within a person's psyche or memory as the person reflects on or dreams about one who is deceased. The source of the message is not the deceased person, but rather God. For example, in dreams, messages originate with God and/or with memories and come to a sleeping person in ways that can be understood, sometimes though "conversation" with a deceased person.

26. Carroll Saussy and Barbara J. Clarke, "The Healing Power of Anger," in *Through the Eyes of Women: Insights for Pastoral Care*, ed. Jeanne Stevenson Moessner (Minneapolis: Fortress Press, 1996), 107.

27. Eugene Peterson, *Five Smooth Stones for Pastoral Work* (Grand Rapids, Mich.: Eerdmans, 1980), 142.

28. Ron Guengerich is a Mennonite minister in Archbold, Ohio, and an adjunct professor at AMBS.

29. Peterson, 143.

30. Ibid., 145.

31. John Rempel, ed., *Minister's Manual* (Newton, Kan.: Faith & Life Press, 1998), 183.

32. J. David Pleins, *The Psalms: Songs of Tragedy, Hope and Justice* (Maryknoll, N.Y.: Orbis, 1993), 91, 13, 92.

33. Elaine Ramshaw, *Ritual and Pastoral Care* (Philadelphia: Fortress Press, 1987), 22.

34. Wayne E. Oates, *Grief, Transition, and Loss: A Pastor's Practical Guide* (Minneapolis: Fortress Press, 1997), 26.

35. Wayne E. Oates, *Pastoral Care and Counseling in Grief and Separation* (Philadelphia: Fortress Press, 1976), 62-75.

36. Kenneth R. Mitchell and Herbert Anderson, *All Our Losses, All Our Griefs: Resources for Pastoral Care* (Philadelphia: Westminster Press, 1983).

37. Tom F. Driver, *Liberating Rites: Understanding the Transformative Power of Ritual* (Boulder, Colo.: Westview, 1998), 166.

38. Ibid., 80.

39. Ibid., 166.

40. Paul E. Irion, "Ritual Responses to Death," in *Living with Grief: At Work, at School, at Worship,* eds. Joyce D. Davidson and Kenneth J. Doka, Hospice Foundation of America (Levittown, Pa.: Brunner/Mazel, 1999), 157.

41. Peg Elliott Mayo and David Feinstein, *Rituals for Living and Dying: How We Can Turn Loss and the Fear of Death into an Affirmation of Life* (HarperSanFrancisco, 1990), 132-71.

42. Therese A. Rando, *Grief, Dying and Death: Clinical Interventions for Caregivers* (Champaign, Ill.: Research Press Company, 1984), 104.

43. Ibid., 105-6.

44. Driver, 212.

45. Ibid., 190.

46. The Linns are Roman Catholics with associations to a Jesuit community in Minneapolis. Two of their many books are *Sleeping with Bread: Holding What Gives You Life* (New York, Paulist Press, 1995) and *Remembering Our Home: Healing Hurts and Receiving Gifts from Conception to Birth* (New York, Paulist Press, 1999).

47. James M. Lapp, "On Losing a Spouse," *Christian Living,* June 2000, 24.

48. These were questions 4 and 5 in the Living Well Questionnaire. Question 4 presented options to check, including "other," under which some people specified "God," which was not one of the options listed. Question 5 was a yes/no question with an open-ended "If so, how?" following.

49. The man who was the pastor is no longer in pastoral ministry.

50. Sara Wengerd, *A Healing Grief: Walking with Your Friend Through Loss* (Scottdale, Pa.: Herald Press, 2002), 39-61 passim.

51. Lynn Kelly, *Don't Ask for a Dead Man's Golf Clubs: What to Do and Say (and What Not to) When a Friend Loses a Loved One* (New York: Workman, 2000).

52. Neuger, 4.

53. Stephen R. Shuchter and Sidney Zisook, "The Therapeutic Tasks of Grief," in *Biopsychosocial Aspects of Bereavement,* ed. Sidney Zisook (Washington D.C.: American Psychiatric Press, 1987), 177-89.

54. Jean Stairs, *Listening for the Soul: Pastoral Care and Spiritual Direction* (Minneapolis: Fortress, 2000), 82.

55. John D. Rempel, "Eternity Sunday Celebrates the Close of the Church Year," *Mennonite Reporter,* vol. 18, no. 19 (September 26, 1988), 9. Rempel states that Eternity Sunday (the last Sunday of the liturgical year) can fill "a gap in Protestant pastoral life, addressing death in a theologically consistent way and lifting up the church as the communion of the living and the dead." This service does not "make a distinction between 'saints' and other Christians; [the] prayers for the dead [are] ones of thanks rather than intercession."

56. A responsive reading for Eternity Sunday/Memorial Sunday/All Saints' Day is in *Hymnal Worship Book,* ed. Rebecca Slough (Scottdale, Pa.: Mennonite Publishing House, 1992), 805.

57. John D. Rempel, ed., *Minister's Manual* (Newton, Kan., and Winnipeg, Man.: Faith & Life Press; Scottdale, Pa., and Waterloo, Ont.: Herald Press, 1998), 134.

58. Ibid., 129-32.

59. Marlene Kropf and Eddy Hall, *Praying with the Anabaptists: The Secret of Bearing Fruit* (Newton, Kan.: Faith & Life Press, 1994), 69.

60. Earl A. Grollman, "The Clergyman's Role in Grief Counseling," in *Community Mental Health: The Role of Church and Temple*, ed. Howard J. Clinebell Jr. (Nashville: Abingdon Press, 1970), 98.

Conclusion

1. Julian of Norwich, *Showings* (also called *Revelations of Divine Love*), trans. Edmund Colledge, OSA, and James Walsh, SJ (New York: Paulist Press, 1978), 315.

2. Grace M. Jantzen, *Julian of Norwich: Mystic and Theologian* (Mahwah, N.J.: Paulist Press, 2000), viii.

3. This is the e-mailed version of the questionnaire. The questionnaire that was sent by mail was in booklet form and had spaces for responses.

Scriptural References

Genesis 38:6-10 . . . . 229 (note 81)

Jeremiah 31:15 63

Jeremiah 31:22b 62

Psalm 22:1 . . . . 55, 170

Psalm 54:1 55

Psalm 73:23 51

Song of Solomon 5:5 . . . . 229 (note 81)

Matthew 2:18 63

Matthew 5:27-28 150

Matthew 19:4-6 123

Luke 1:52-53 175

Luke 18 63

John 12:24 . . . . 11, 69

Romans 5:3-4 48

1 Corinthians 2:10 84

1 Corinthians 13:12 40

Index

After-death "communication," 167-68
All Saints' Day, 170-72, 190
Alone, 33-34, 72-74, 89-90, 101, 108, 119, 131, 191, 215
Alter, Margaret, 161, 165-66
AMBS (Associated Mennonite Biblical Seminary), 13, 14, 16, 25, 100, 155, 197
Anger, 26, 53, 55, 57, 76, 87, 89, 96, 168-69
Attachment to deceased spouse, 121, 132
Augustine of Hippo, 83, 128-29, 140

Barth, Karl, 53
Bell, John L., 209
Billman, Kathleen D., 132, 169
Blair, Pamela D., 213
Bonhoeffer, Dietrich, 37, 41, 46
Brothers, Joyce, 146, 150-51, 209
Brown, Gabrielle, 139-40
Brueggemann, Walter, 53, 56, 57, 58

Caregiving sage, 159
Catholic Church, Vatican's Declaration on Sexual Ethics, 142
Celibacy, 130-52, 191
    definitions, 130-31, 230 (note 100)
Celtic spirituality, 129
Charts with information from Living Well Study, 95, 110, 113, 115, 117, 120

Chittister, Joan, 25-26, 48, 61, 77-78, 87, 98, 209
Clark, Keith, 123
Confidentiality, 14, 31, 188, 198
Courting—see dating/courting

Dark night, 62, 87, 195
Dating/courting/romantic relationships, 115-19, 122, 152, 204, 226
Death
    anticipated, 26-27,
    accepting the reality of, 73
    first anniversary of, 176-78
    unexpected/sudden, 26, 29, 81, 114, 198
Death and Sex and Spirituality, 127-28
Degriefing, 30, 218
Devers, Edie, 167-68
DeVries, Robert, 216
Divorce following remarriage, 114, 118
Dreams about the deceased, 167-68
Driedger, Leo, 143
Driver, Tom F., 172-73, 175
Dyck, Gordon, 64

Edelman, Hope, 209
Ericsson, Stephanie, 210
Erikison, Erik, 123
Eternity Sunday, 170, 190, 233 (note 55)

Fantasy, sexual, 146, 149-51
Feinberg. Linda, 210

Felber, Marta, 210
Ferris, Frank D., 212
First and second years after spousal death, 94-97
First anniversary of death, see Death, First anniversary of
Fitzgerald, Helen, 210
Foster, Richard, 111, 123, 127, 149
Frankl, Victor, 27, 37, 48, 56, 76
Freud, Sigmund, 86, 132, 135-36
Friendships, 106, 107-12, 123, 133-35, 136, 145, 155-56, 157, 178-87, 205-6
Funerals, 60, 164-65, 170-71, 189

Gender vs. sex, 219 (note 20)
Genitality, 112, 122, 126, 134, 136-37, 142, 144-45
Gibran, Kahlil, 21, 46
Gifts of grief, 50, 75, 85, 97-98, 126, 160, 177-78, 195, 202
Ginsburg, Genevieve Davis, 210
God,
    relationship with, 37-41, 58, 79-89, 106, 111, 130, 139, 158, 162, 169, 200
    wrestling with, 37-38
Goergen, Donald, 126, 129-30, 137
Going inward/deep within, 34, 86, 92, 134-36, 152, 159, 189, 192, 193-94
Graham, Sylvester, 141
Greenblatt, Stephen, 141
Grief—definitions, 52
    tasks of grief, see Mourning, tasks of
    "getting over" grief, 12, 62, 65-68, 185, 201
    immobilizing grief, 94, 170
Grollman, Earl, 192, 211
Guengerich, Ron, 169

Hanson, Warren, 211
Haskins, Minnie Louise, 155
Hartzler, Harold E., 5, 12, 17, 24, 36, 99, 100-1

Healing, 75-76, 93-94, 156-57, 167, 169-70, 173, 175, 187, 192
Healing Grief: Walking with Your Friend Through Loss, A, 187, 215
Hershberger, Ann, 124
Heschel, Abraham, 38
Hicks, John Mark, 211
Hillel, Rabbi, 162
Hope, 25-26, 40-41, 43-49, 58, 60, 62-63, 65, 76, 77-78, 158-59, 163, 170, 177, 192, 194-95
Hostetter, Sherill, 22

Identity, 12, 36, 72, 86, 98-101, 136, 195
Inconsummation, 52, 131, 137-38
Integration of loss, 29, 78, 80, 89-92, 94, 101, 169, 188, 195
Integration of Sexuality, Heart, Head, and Spirituality, 15, 138-39
Intimacy,
    with God, 84, 88, 105, 111, 125-27
    with others, 34, 81, 84, 105, 106-7, 111-12, 120, 123, 124-27, 136-37, 145-49

Jones, Doris Moreland, 29, 211
Joy and sorrow, 45-46, 62, 75, 98, 189, 195
Joyce, Mary Rosera, 123, 127, 131, 133-36
Joyce, Robert, 123, 127, 131
Julian of Norwich, 193-95

Kauffman, J. Howard, 143
Kellogg, J., 141
Kidd, Sue Monk, 62, 211
Klassen, Otto D., 9-10, 16, 35
Koontz, Gayle Gerber, 164
Kotva, Joseph, 151
Krabill, Willard, 107, 124
Kropf, Marlene, 46, 191
Kübler-Ross, Elisabeth, 53, 68
Kushner, Harold, 41, 42-43, 211

Lambin, Helen Reichert, 212
Lament, 51-76
    definition, 52
    in the church year, 61-63
    in worship, 54, 169-72
Lamentations, 63, 50
Lapp, James, 176
Laqueur, Thomas, 140-41
L'Engle, Madeleine, 58, 212
"Letting go," 73-74
Levang, Elizabeth, 116, 212
Lewis, C. S., 29, 42, 57-58, 65,
    106, 131, 212
Life and death questions/issues/
    mysteries of, 13, 25, 27-28,
    78, 81-82, 91, 98, 156, 163
Liminal/Liminality, 77, 78-80,
    172, 175, 190
Linn, Dennis, Matthew, and Sheila
    Fabricant, 84, 175
Liturgy of death, 164, 169-72
Livengood, Gale, 26
Living Well Questionnaire/Study,
    14, 31, 54, 58, 66-67, 85, 87,
    94-95, 99, 108, 110, 112-13,
    115, 116-17, 119, 122, 124,
    132, 138, 146, 148-49, 155,
    160, 185, 187, 197-207
Loder, James E., 29, 83, 86, 92,
    101-2, 125, 127
Loneliness, 33, 66, 82, 89-92,
    105, 119, 122, 191
Longing for God, 107, 111, 126
Longing for union, 111
L'Onanisme, 141
*Loss as an Invitation to
Transformation: Living Well
Following the Death of a
Spouse,* 14

Manning, Doug, 212, 216
Marriage, 30, 85-86, 106-7, 119-
    22, 124-25, 131
Marriage after widowhood, 67-
    68, 74, 114, 118, 203-4
Martin, John D., 212
Maslow, Abraham, 136-37
Masturbation, 140-46, 149-52
Mayo, Peg Elliott, 28, 173

Mennonite(s), 32, 143, 217, 237
Mennonite Church publications,
    143-45
Migliore, Daniel L., 132, 169
Miller, James, E., 162,
Moffat, Mary Jane, 213
Moltmann, Jürgen, 37, 40
Mourning
    definition, 52
    tasks of mourning, 59, 68-75,
    99, 159, 173, 188, 201
Mystery, 30-31, 39-40, 45, 58, 79,
    91

Narrative Pastoral Counseling,
    158-59
Natural disasters, 24, 26, 42, 54
Nelson, James, 123
Neufeld, Elsie K., 27, 213
New relationships, see Dating/
    courting/romantic relation-
    ships
Newell, J. Philip, 128-29
Noel, Brook, 213
Norris, Kathleen, 78, 133,
Nouwen, Henri J. M., 34, 45-48,
    130-31, 160-61, 163-64, 213-
    14
Nueger, Christie Cozad, 158-59

Oates, Wayne, 28, 171-72
Ollenburger, Ben, 24
Orgasm, 127, 137, 145, 148

Pastoral care, 97, 155-92, 195
Peachey, Lorne, 143
Pelagius, 128-29
Peterson, Eugene, 33, 50, 169-70
Plan for pastoral care for bereaved
    people, 187-92
Pleins, J. David, 56, 171
Pornography, 230-31 (note 111)
Postema, Don, 38
Prashant, Lyn, 22, 30, 49
"Praying goodbyes," 70, 159, 214
"Praying Mantis," 128
Presbyterian General Assembly
    booklet, 142
Psalm 73:23, 51

Questionnaire (see Living Well Questionnaire)

Ramshaw, Elaine, 171
Rando, Therese, 173-75,
Regrets about new relationships, 118, 204
Relationships
　with God, 106
　with others, see Friendships or Dating/courting/romantic relationships
Remarriage, 67-68, 74, 114, 203-4
　triadic relationships in remarriage, 121
Rempel, John D., 170
Rituals, 70, 163-64, 167, 170-78, 189, 191-92
Rolheiser, Ronald, 39, 52, 92, 122-23, 127, 138, 151
Rosenau, Douglas, 149-50
Rupp, Joyce, 70, 80-81, 159, 214

Schipani, Daniel S., 16, 159, 198
Shuchter, Stephen R., 148, 188
Schweibert, Pat, 214
Second marriage—see marriage after widowhood
Self-actualization, 136-37
Self-care for caregivers, 162-63
September 11, 2001, 23, 24, 25, 52
Sex/sexuality, Latin root/definitions, 111, 122-24
Sexual energy, 132-40, 148, 195, 206, 228 (note 62)
Sexual expression, 128, 134-35
Sexual repression, 133-36
Sexual sublimation; 135, 137-39
Sexuality, 15, 30, 86-87, 103-52, 206-7, 228
Sexuality and Spirituality, see Spirituality and Sexuality
Shaw, Luci, 214
Sittser, Gerald, 42, 43, 214
Smith, Harold Ivan, 214
Socializing, 90-91
Soelle, Dorothee, 44

Sorrow and joy, see Joy and sorrow
Spiritual direction/spiritual director, 82, 157-58, 163
Spirituality and Sexuality, 125-27, 148
Spousal sanctification, 121-22
Stages of dying, 53, 68-69
Stairs, Jean, 39-40
Staten, Henry, 127-28
Struggling, 25, 45, 48-49, 51, 61-62, 81-82
Support after spousal death, 67, 96, 108-9, 178-87
Swartley, Willard M., 42

Thatcher, Adrian, 141-42, 150
Thesis project, 13-14, 16, 194, 197-207
Thomas, Everett, 143
Timing for new relationships/marriage, 112-19, 121
Timing of grief/mourning, 93-97
Tissot, 141
Transformation, 29, 37, 43, 47, 49, 51, 58-59, 62, 70, 74, 77-90, 98-102, 172, 192, 194-95
Trinity, 106
Tripp, David, 164

Union/one flesh, 29, 30, 123, 125, 130, 139
Union with God, 83, 84, 107, 111, 125, 139
U.S. census, 117, 217

Vacuum, 83-84, 93
Viorst, Judith, 83- 84
Voice, coming to voice/finding one's voice, 52, 58, 92, 101, 158
Voice of God, 192

Way of Wisdom, The, 159-60
Wedding ring, 101, 147
Weems, Ann, 169, 215
Wengerd, Sara, 187, 215

Whitehead, Evelyn and James, 145, 149
Wiebe, Katie Funk, 101, 215
Wiesel, Elie, 39
Wife to widow to woman, 100
Wolfelt, Alan, 51
Wolterstorff, Nicholas, 42-43, 45, 47, 215
Worship, 34-35, 54-59, 61-62, 86, 164, 170-71
Wounded healer, 47, 156, 160-62

Yaguchi, Yorifumi, 128
Yoder, Perry, 41

Zonnebelt-Smeege, Susan, 67, 215-16

The Author

Rachel Nafziger Hartzler at age fifty-one endured the unrelenting sorrow and confusion of widowhood after her husband died suddenly of a heart attack. While studying for a master's degree in Christian formation at Associated Mennonite Biblical Seminary, she undertook to research the experiences of other widowed people. Hartzler has taught nursing at Goshen (Indiana) College and practiced nursing at Goshen General Hospital. She currently works as a spiritual director, speaks on issues related to grief, spirituality, and sexuality, and is pastor of Pleasant Oaks Mennonite Church in Middlebury, Indiana. She lives with her daughters in Goshen and visits her grandchildren in North Carolina as often as possible.